SMALL BUSINESS WORKS!

Eugene L. Gross, Adrian R. Cancel, Oscar Figueroa

SMALL BUSINESS WORKS!

How to compete and win in the free enterprise system

Illustrated by Eugene L. Gross

amacom

A division of American Management Associations

ST. PHILIPS COLLEGE LIBRARY

658.022
G878

Library of Congress Cataloging in Publication Data

Gross, Eugene L
   Small business works!

   Includes index.
   1. Business. 2. Small business. I. Cancel,
Adrian R., joint author. II. Figueroa, Oscar,
1949-   joint author. III. Title.
HF5500.G78   658'.022   ~~77-23471~~
ISBN 0-8144-5443-7

© 1977 AMACOM
A division of American Management Associations, New York.
All rights reserved. Printed in the United States of America.

This publication may not be reproduced, stored in a retrieval system,
or transmitted in whole or in part, in any form or by any means, electronic, mechanical, photocopying, recording, or otherwise, without
the prior written permission of AMACOM, 135 West 50th Street, New
York, N.Y. 10020.

First Printing

Dedicated

to the small-business people of the world,
who pull a heavy load.

57522

PREFACE

The Businessman and Businesswoman

Small-business people contribute heavily to the success of the economy and to other businesses, professionals, and workers.

As employers, as customers of other businesses, as taxpayers, as community developers and providers of services, as promoters of the free enterprise system, the over 9 million small businesses are in many ways the very foundation of democracy, proving that opportunity is there for those who seek it and are willing to work hard to find success.

Manufacturers, suppliers, distributors, wholesalers, service businesses, professional services, repair and maintenance, and other technical businesses all benefit from the small-business sector and in many ways depend on its success and survival.

However, if small-business operators fail, they can only turn to their family or close friends for comfort. Business is a jungle, and only the fittest survive.

Despite the contribution of small business, each small-business person stands alone and must protect his or her interests as best possible.

A thorough understanding of business—awareness of changes, trends, and needs inside and outside the business, and management

skills—is most often the difference between business success and failure.

Small-business people carry an enormous burden. They make many unusual sacrifices in order to succeed. Those who profit from their endeavors are happy to receive the benefits. On the other hand, if things turn sour and the business declines, workers will seek other jobs and dealers will find other customers.

Small-business operators may lose their investment, the time spent trying to build a business, and their chances to try again. They can end up in serious debt.

That burden must be respected. It takes courage to go into business.

Eugene L. Gross
Adrian R. Cancel
Oscar Figueroa

Contents

ST. PHILIPS COLLEGE LIBRARY

1

Introduction

Are you operating in the dark? Have you lost touch with your business? Your markets? Your industry? Labor? Are you aware of the changes going on around you, in your business and outside? Do you know how they affect you?

Within your own operation you can initiate changes, but you can only react to outside changes. How do you react?

The potential for success is measured by the ability of a business to respond to changes and needs, both external and internal. Those businesses which respond tend to succeed. Those which cannot or do not respond tend to decline and fail.

A great many businesspeople, although aware of this, are locked in by day-to-day pressures and demands and do not take the time to monitor changes and needs, to study their effects, and to plan measures to deal with them. Generally, they first become aware of the effects when trouble develops. Often it is too late, and remedy is costly. In the meantime, aggressive competition may have taken advantage of the situation and grabbed up most of the sales.

All business people must combine entrepreneurial and managerial traits, but different situations require different emphases. There comes a time in the growth of every business when sound management must be given more attention than rapid expansion and risk taking.

Good businesspeople must also be smart businesspeople, for

How many hats do you wear? How many heads do you have? Few businesspeople can be shop foreman, bookkeeper, shipping and receiving clerk, machine operator, purchasing agent, and manager—all rolled into one—and still do right for the business.

good is not always good enough. They must know their businesses, operations, industries, markets, and the general economy and keep in constant touch with them. They must be aware of problems and changes and have a sound understanding of business principles. Where do you stand on these points?

Sound management must respond intelligently to change by getting the facts, analyzing them, defining alternative actions, evaluating the business resources, selecting a course of action and implementing it. That requires a broad business knowledge and experience.

Few businesspeople can be economist, financial analyst and cost accountant, marketing and merchandising specialist, production and systems expert, all rolled into one.

Big business employs teams of specialists to identify changes and needs, to develop plans and strategies to convert resources into business advantages, to respond to change, and to seize opportunities.

Small business, which includes most of the businesses in the United States, cannot support such professional staffs. Yet it needs the same kinds of professional inputs.

You can go out into the professional marketplace and buy those inputs—*or* you can learn how to help yourself meet many of your own needs. You can learn to identify changes and needs, to evaluate them, to research them, and to plan to maximize your resources and opportunities. Read on and find out how.

Business comprises many functional units of operation, such as management, marketing, production, purchasing, sales, and finance. Anything that affects one unit affects all. The smart businessperson constantly makes adjustments in all operating units to direct the effects of change to business advantage and ensure a sound business balance.

Businesses must buy goods or services and sell goods or services. If, for example, your raw materials or other supplies become more expensive, this means that your costs for goods sold go up. However, consumers may react to price adjustments, markets can be lost, and sales and profits may drop. By the same token, if goods or materials are in short supply, costs may rise, production may fall off, sales drop, profits dip, and so on.

If interest rates increase, money becomes expensive, financing becomes difficult, working capital shrinks, collections slow down, and capacities to produce and deliver diminish. Changes in consumer preferences and lifestyles can change demand, alter markets, and cut sales.

When changes threaten sales, markets, production, or financing, businesspeople must make adjustments to restore a sound balance. Their constant task is to try to reduce costs, increase profits, expand their capabilities to respond to change, and seize opportunities for business advantage.

If they develop their professional skills, business people can learn to identify changes and needs, define their effects on their businesses, and adjust operations so as to restore a good balance between their resources and their competitive position in the marketplace.

All businesspeople walk a tightrope each business day. Changes are constantly going on inside and outside businesses, and they must be dealt with effectively. There are no business secrets for success. Business understanding is the single most important requirement for business survival.

Businesspeople who can understand the interrelationships of all operational units, functions, and responsibilities can identify the adjustments and techniques that are most likely to restore the stability and profitability of the business.

Businesses simply do not take care of themselves. To be successful, they require informed and responsive management. And to fulfill its obligations, management must develop the required skills and understanding and institute controls that will insure stable and profitable operation over a long term.

Business planning, whether short-range or long-range, must consider not only the resources of the business, current operations, and financial needs, but also the changes and needs that can affect the business now and in the future.

This book is designed to help all people in business understand the mechanics of business operation, the interrelationships of operational units, and provide them with the techniques, skills, sources of data, and sensitivity needed to identify changes and respond to them effectively.

2

Management

Most small businesses were started by entrepreneurs. Entrepreneurs are persons with some knowledge or skill in a business field, and some funds, who take the risk of venturing into business in various states of preparedness or unpreparedness.

In the process of choosing a business area, deciding definitely to go into business, and going through all the agonies of getting the business started, entrepreneurs have few people to turn to for support and comfort. They tend to be loners, self-dependent people characterized by a slight mistrust of other businesspeople and workers.

They keep their affairs to themselves, make all decisions, and carry the sole burden for all aspects of business operation. They often view their employees as bodies without minds, who must be told what to do at all times. Entrepreneurs tend to be dictatorial.

That strong self-reliance distorts reason, and most entrepreneurs think they know everything about everything to do with their business. This, above all other causes, is the prime factor in business failure.

Many times businesses are started by entrepreneurs with reasonably good experience in only one phase of a total operation, perhaps as salesmen or supervisors or even as production workers. The mere act of going into their own business does not magically give them instant knowledge and understanding of all other aspects of a business operation. Entrepreneurs must find complementary and supplementary skills and experience in their associates and their employees

Listen to your business through management lines of communication.

if their businesses are to be properly serviced, controlled, and managed.

One person with limited experience cannot wear 50 hats and expect to do the business any good. A former salesman, now a business owner, may sell up a storm, but without skills in production he may find every sale a losing proposition.

When entrepreneurs accept the fact that they do not know everything, and either employ or work with people who know what they don't know about the business; when they trust them to use their skills and experience intelligently for the good of the business, with responsibility and accountability, then and only then do they become business managers and can they succeed.

A growing business needs management more than entrepreneurship. In a management-run business, the owners employ qualified specialists and workers to help them meet all the operational skill requirements of a business and, through systems of communication and control, assign different persons the responsibilities of operating different parts of the business for which they are best prepared.

If the owner cannot afford to employ specialists in all basic operational areas, he or she can get outside help from a variety of sources as and when it is needed.

Each person assigned a specific responsibility by management must be accountable to management and must keep management informed of everything that is going on in, or indirectly affects, that area of responsibility.

In this way, a number of qualified people can intelligently bring specialized knowledge and experience to bear in different operational units, on a full-time and concentrated basis. The sum total of all the separate efforts is far, far greater than what could be achieved by one entrepreneur alone.

Through systems of communication and control, top management has direct lines to middle management, and in turn, middle management has direct lines to workers and to day-to-day operations.

The *chain of command,* with information flowing up and down the lines of communication and control, enables the owners to *manage* the business without physically getting involved, every day of the week, in each operation, each decision, each action. Time is freed for top management to collect data and information through systems, both inside and outside the business, so that it can identify changes and needs that affect the business and its success, and develop plans and strategies for dealing with them.

Keep direct lines of control and communication to all divisions and functional units of your business.

Even if a company has few employees, it needs a chain of command. Responsibilities must be appropriately assigned, and there must be accountability and lines of communication and control so that management can devote time to business analysis, planning, and supervision.

Only a well-managed business can make it in the long run.

Management Controls

If a business is to be successful, its management must have direct lines of control and communication with all operational units.

Management, as we have seen, must constantly make adjustments in response to changes and needs, inside and outside the business. It must be aware of the effects of changes on the different operational units, and how adjustments of one unit will affect the others. If management lacks the ability to adjust the units of the business so as to insure the proper balance, important opportunities will be lost.

Those lines of control and communication require an orderly system. Responsibilities must be clearly assigned, and every member of the organization must be accountable to management. The data required for effective operation must be identified and collected, organized, and reported by qualified people, who must also make the adjustments ordered by management.

Management cannot wear 50 hats or be in 50 places at the same time. It must rely on its employees to provide it with day-to-day information on what is happening in each operational unit. With that knowledge, it can control the business. Without it, it has lost control.

Management must listen to its business. A business is constantly talking to management. Sometimes it has good things to say, and sometimes bad things. Management must listen in good times and bad.

With lines of communication and control, management can accomplish this task. It may hear that the delivery of materials is poor and production suffering. It may hear that customers are resisting because the competition is underselling. It may hear that the costs of goods or materials went up. It may hear that labor is goofing off and production suffers.

When the business complains, it has good reason. Something is wrong. If management does not attend to the trouble, things can get worse. The problem is sure to affect the entire operation. Therefore, when the business and management listen and talk to each other, the business has a far better chance of maintaining stability and profitability.

Because a business is a complex entity, communication and control are not easy. Systems have to be established to insure that all parties are listening to each other and talking to each other.

The same is true for the industry, markets, and the economy. The business must react to changes and needs outside. It needs lines of communication with the outside world.

Although the business has little or no control over the outside world, it must react to things happening outside that affect the business. Unless it can listen to—and *hear*—what is going on outside, it cannot react and must pay the consequences.

Therefore, management must also establish lines of communication with outside agents, which can supply the business with pertinent data that concern its operation, markets, labor supply, supply of materials and goods, and financing, to name a few.

Inside adjustments must be related to outside events and influences. Management must establish both inside and outside lines of communication, as well as inside controls.

It does not matter whether a business has one manager and five employees or 100 in management and 2,000 employees—the same factors are at work, and the same listening and control posts must be established.

To collect critical data about a business, management seeks prime indicators that yield an accurate picture of specific operations or the business as a whole. Lending institutions, suppliers, and other outside parties measure the business by their own indicators, which are based on your indicators. They may or may not lend money or give credit because of those indicators.

Indicators are valuable management tools. They include sales figures, costs of goods sold, unit costs in production, labor costs, prices for products or services, costs of raw materials or supplies, available working capital. Any of these items tells something specific about the business and its units.

In collecting all pertinent data, management can construct a profile of the business, a picture of all operations separately and as a whole, to determine where adjustments can be made, or must be made, to improve stability and profitability.

Management, as we've indicated, must also be concerned about how the business picture looks to outsiders. Banks, for instance, will examine certain business ratios to determine whether or not to lend money to the business. The indicators they use include ratios of assets to liabilities, fixed assets to net worth, debt to net worth, and many others that will be discussed in the section on accounting and finance.

Therefore, management is concerned not only with keeping the business stable and successful, but also with the general image the business projects. That image can bear heavily on the future of any business.

There are also indicators that come from the outside, from governmental and private agencies and sources. They give clues about the economy, markets, consumers, products and services, materials and supplies. These indicators are of great importance to management since they reveal changes outside to which management must react. Also, they identify many new opportunities for investigation and development. Management cannot afford to ignore these outside indicators.

Of course, every business is unique in some way. It has its own particular markets and products or services. Some highly specialized businesses, which service very specialized and singular aspects of industries or markets, may have their own special indicators as well as those described above. Yet, all business requires the same basic management techniques.

The Structure of the Business

In business, time is money. If something essential to the operation of the business can be done well in less time, then it costs less. The owners or management, together with the employees, must do all the work needed to operate the business. The more work they can do in a given time, the greater the productivity will be and the lower the costs. Cost savings often mean higher profits.

If people are given jobs that they don't understand or for which they have insufficient training or experience, the work could take much longer than if done by a trained and experienced person. Even if somebody who lacks the proper experience worked for less money, the fact that it took so much time to do the job may make that job cost more than if done by an experienced person paid more money.

In business there are many jobs to be done; they're commonly called *functions*. Functions are steps in the business process. For instance, in retailing, goods must be ordered, received, priced, stocked, displayed, sold, packaged, billed, and often delivered. Records must also be kept for all steps. All of the steps, including the billing and record keeping, are functions. The same holds true for all steps in manufacturing, supply, repair, and service or professional businesses.

When related functions are grouped together, the result is called an *operational unit,* **or** *functional unit.*

A functional unit may include all ordering of materials or goods, receiving and checking of materials and goods from suppliers and manufacturers, taking inventory of goods with codes, stocking of shelves, pricing of received goods, marking of goods, and inventory maintenance. Also included in the same functional unit would be records of goods ordered, goods received, amounts of inventory, and prices.

Functional units are made up of related functions so that persons with special training or experience can service them better in less time.

One experienced person can service many related functions, and service them well. When the work load is heavy and more people are needed to do the job, the one best experienced and trained can supervise other workers, each of whom will be doing what he or she knows best.

The functional unit's supervisor or manager, even if that unit consists of a single person, is responsible for a set of functions, all of which are important steps in the business process. In businesses where the entrepreneur has not learned to be a manager, functions probably haven't been defined clearly, functional units have not been structured, and all functional responsibility is vested in one person—the entrepreneur.

A functional organization chart of this business would look like this:

```
ENTREPRENEUR
Sales
Finance
Marketing
Production
. . .
```

The employees of such a company are mere bodies, without assigned functions. They're not part of functional units and have no responsibility for doing the best job in the shortest time.

Having no responsibility to see a job function through or to make decisions about the work, they must always wait for the entrepreneur to make decisions. If the entrepreneur is busy or not available, the job is held up. Time is lost. Money is lost.

In the entrepreneurial situation, workers tend to perform all kinds of unrelated functions. When businesses use all labor for all functions, there is no way to determine the costs of specific functions. Therefore, it becomes impossible to operate any system of cost control or institute cost-saving practices.

Organizing the business in terms of functions and functional units helps measure costs. The costs of all functional units represent the total cost of operating the business. With such an approach, it becomes easy to identify the costs of specific functions and the relationship of functions to profits. If costs can be reduced for any function or functional unit, profits will rise.

If changes inside or outside the business affect the costs of labor or supplies, or the costs of doing business (taxes, insurance), management can examine the functional units to determine which are affected by those changes and seek ways to reduce costs in functional units so affected. In other words, breaking down operational steps into functions and functional units is a way to control a business, costs, and productivity.

Each function requires the labor of someone. It could be provided by employees or by outside experts such as accountants, lawyers, or consultants. Even if a function is serviced by outside experts—whether it is for a fee or free of charge—that function exists and must be included in the functional units.

The assignment of actual employees to functional areas is the *staffing organization*. The staffing organization defines specific tasks within specific functional units to specific persons. It fixes responsibilities, accountability, and standards of performance and establishes chains of command. Each functional unit has a manager who answers to top management. Each functional-unit manager is responsible for those persons working in his or her functional unit.

A functional organization chart for a management-run business may look like Figure 1. The chart lists principal functional units and under them those functions which are most critical to the business process. This provides a clear picture of the main functional concerns of a company.

The staffing chart for a management-run business may look like Figure 2. Such a chart identifies the people in each functional unit, even those who are not employees, like the accountant and the person from the outside advertising company.

The functional and staffing charts are maps of the business process. They are the basis for analyzing the costs and the productivity of the business. With these maps, management can make adjustments to meet many different business needs.

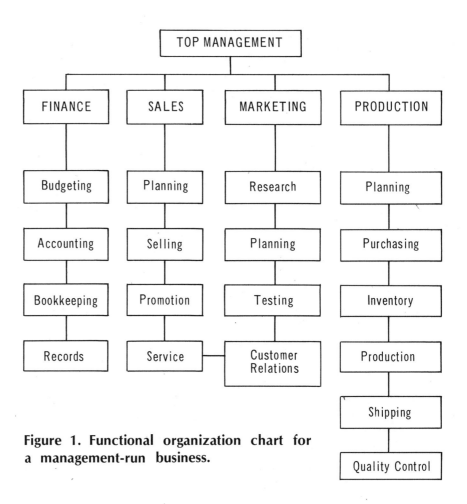

Figure 1. Functional organization chart for a management-run business.

Functional and staffing charts illustrate the functional units for easy evaluation; the persons working within those units for easy identification; non-employees contributing to the performance of functions within functional units; the chain of command; and the lines of communication and control.

Comparing the functional organizational chart of the entrepreneur-run business with that of the management-run business, we can easily see that the entrepreneur's chart does not break down the functions or units or assign workers to functions, whereas the charts of the management-run business do. This reflects the differences in concepts, awareness, and business understanding between the entrepreneur and the manager. A management-run business has control. An entrepreneur-run business has little control.

Regardless of size or number of employees, all businesses must break down all functions in the business process and organize them into functional units, even if certain functions are serviced by

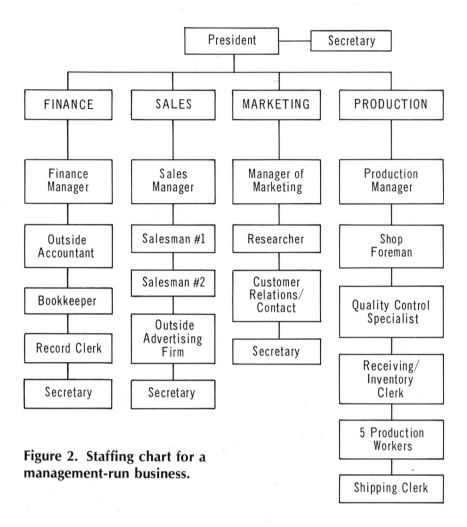

Figure 2. Staffing chart for a management-run business.

persons outside the business. Staffing charts must show all people performing functions, even if they are not employees.

Outside labor may include professional services, such as those provided by accountants, lawyers, technicians, or other businesses that do specific work related to various functional units. Such services may be purchased or obtained free from governmental or private agencies serving small-business people. Also, some functions may be farmed out to other businesses, which may handle sales, advertising, marketing, finance, or other jobs for your company.

Sometimes outside labor noted in the staffing charts will be replaced by full-time employees of the company. For instance, when a company gets large enough, it may find that it is more economical and efficient to hire a full-time accountant instead of working with an outside accountant.

By including each and every function, and each and every person providing services to functional units, management can tell what work has to be done in the course of business and how many people it takes to do it—and how many people are being paid to do it. In short, functional and staffing charts are essential tools for control, planning, and adjustment to change.

Performance Standards

Using the functional and staffing charts, management can determine what work has to be done, what skills workers or professionals must have to do it, and how much work they must do for what cost.

If a functional chart shows a need for an accountant, management knows that it must employ a person with training and experience as an accountant. If the business operates in very specialized fields, it may seek an accountant with experience in accounting in those special fields. It must pay the accountant a salary at least equal to market rates for the experience and training. Therefore, in planning and budgeting operational costs, it becomes possible to identify specific business needs and costs.

If the business needs a machine operator for a particular machine, it must seek someone with experience and training in the operation of that kind of machinery. It must pay the market wage-rate for the machine operator, or union rates if the business is a union shop. Furthermore, it must make a profit on the machine operator, and not just recover wages, taxes, and other costs attributed to carrying the operator on the payroll.

In order for the business to make a profit on the operator, the operator must produce enough work to cover more than his or her costs and expenses. Therefore, in identifying a need for a machine operator, and in planning and budgeting costs, the amount of work that the machine operator must produce becomes an important consideration.

Standards of performance and qualification directly describe the function to be served and the functional unit to which it belongs; the training, skills, and experience needed to fill the function; the expected productivity of the person who will fill the function; and the point at which that person no longer contributes to the profitability of the business.

Sometimes an employee need not make a profit to be valuable and needed. Certain functions in the business may be needed to make the operation run soundly, even though they do not in themselves directly contribute to profitability. For instance, a person in a retail operation who handles returns, while serving a necessary function, does not directly contribute to profits like a salesman. However, for customer relations such a function and person are needed.

Labor must be tailor-made to functions and costs.

Too many people performing functions that do not directly contribute to the profitability of a business can become an operational burden and cut seriously into profits, thereby endangering business success. This generally happens in larger businesses, which employ large numbers of workers.

Management must look for the perfect match of function and person to fill it.

In order to fill a function with the best-qualified person, and to maximize the returns to the business in terms of productivity and profits, management must clearly identify the training, skills, and experience a person should have to do the best job. Also, it should check with employment agencies or the classified ads in the papers to get an idea of fair wages or salaries for that job. In this way, it can compute its costs for employing the person, and its expected returns.

Management must tell employees exactly what it expects them to do, and how.

Whereas management has identified functions and staff slots to be filled, and clearly understands the skills needed and the costs associated with different positions, most often the employees hired do not clearly understand what they are needed for, what they should be doing, how much is expected of them, and how they fit into their functional units, the staffing organization, and the business process in general. Without a clear understanding of these things, no employee can successfully fill a function or job slot and do justice to the business.

Management looks for the best match.

Established job standards and qualifications are like contracts. When both management and employee clearly understand what the employee is hired to do, what is expected, and how the employee fits into the business process, they have entered into an agreement. Management offers the job under certain conditions, and the worker accepts those conditions.

In this way there are no misunderstandings. Management needs certain functions filled. It has a staff slot to fill those functions and hires an employee under certain clear conditions to do the job. If the employee does not live up to the accepted conditions, there are clear grounds for dismissal. If the worker does much more than expected, there are good grounds for advancement.

Also, and most important, management knows that it has provided the staff needed to fill certain functions, as planned and budgeted for the business process. It has control.

Information flow to top management.

Job standards and qualifications are prepared from the staffing chart. In addition, *job descriptions* cover all the functions, noted in the functional chart, that go with the job.

Any job slot may entail more than one function. Those different functions should be spelled out in the job description, which goes with the standards and qualifications to form a package, so that all parties know what is expected and what standards have been set.

All parties in a business should know what their job is and what is expected. This avoids confusion and conflict. Also, it fixes responsibility and accountability for functions. It is easy to identify the people responsible for certain functions and to evaluate their performance and productivity. It is easy to compute the relative costs of functions and the contribution of functions to business efficiency and profitability. It enables management to make adjustments in response to change, since it knows the capabilities of its employees and can determine how they can be shifted to different or new staffing slots or assigned to different or new functions. Job descriptions, standards, and qualifications are important tools in management and planning.

The Chain of Command

As noted in previous sections, businesspeople cannot be experts in all business fields, and they can get lost in day-to-day operations. They must set aside time to monitor the business, analyze it, and adjust to changes and needs.

As illustrated in the functional chart and staffing chart, it takes many functions and functional units and different skills and experience to construct a going business. Since businesspeople cannot know everything about each professional field or technical aspect of a business, they must employ the best people they can find to fulfill particular functions, or sets of functions, within the business process.

In order for business owners to keep in touch with all the different functions and people in the organization, they must establish lines of communication and control. They do this by making certain individuals responsible for functions or functional units, and those individuals then become accountable to the business owners for the performance of the staff and the fulfillment of functions. They are responsible for maintaining the level of performance established in the employee standards and qualifications previously described.

Thus, a worker may have certain assigned functions and be part of a functional unit and at the same time be an agent for ownership, or a *manager*. Managers are generally selected because of their training, skills, and experience. Placed in charge of a function or functional unit, they supervise and monitor the work of other employees assigned to that function or unit, and are responsible for the proper fulfillment of the function, or the functions in the unit.

If a business has many functional units, a manager may be appointed to supervise and be responsible for several units, or a *division*. In these cases, the managers of the separate functional units are responsible to the divisional manager. The divisional managers may in turn be responsible to the business owner or to the president of the company. They must be accountable for the performance of all functions and people in the functional units they manage.

Managers, as agents for ownership or top management, think like owners and protect the interests of owners.

Managers must see that workers in the functional areas they supervise are doing what they were hired to do, are doing it well, and are not wasting materials or goods. They see to it that other workers produce at levels established in the employee standards set by ownership or top management. They report on productivity and performance to the managers above them.

Managers must be alert to problems and trouble spots and report to managers above them anything that can affect the fulfillment of functions or the costs of fulfilling them. Such items may be slow delivery of materials needed, high rates of absenteeism, machine failures, receipt of inferior-quality materials or goods, lack of sufficient work to keep other employees busy, abundance of work, or need for additional workers.

Managers must keep records of productivity, costs, labor, and so on and report the pertinent data to managers above them on a regular basis so that their superiors are aware of what is going on in the functional units they manage. Their superiors in turn report to managers above them until all the data, reports, and information reach top management or the owners.

In this way top management or the owners can monitor operations and learn of problems before they become too serious. They can regulate costs of functions and labor and see to it that each function is contributing its share to overall profitability. They can cut waste and maximize resources. They can add or cut labor as needed to keep costs in line with sales. This chain of command is management's line of communication and control.

Reporting

In a good management system everyone is responsible to and reports to somebody higher in the chain of command. Business is controlled through this system of responsibilities and reporting.

Through reporting, good management can take care of problems up and down the line and maintain business stability.

When every employee knows to whom he or she has to report and be responsible to, the lines of communication and control are established. Top management can listen and respond to employees on each level and in each function. Thus, through the system, each person performing a function or group of functions can report on his or her productivity, needs, and problems and also identify ways to improve the process, save costs, or increase efficiency. In major corporations, employee suggestions often result in changes that save millions of dollars in costs or add millions to sales or profits. Big business is smart enough to listen to its workers.

Reporting and responsibility work from the top down too.

When management listens to its workers on all levels and is informed about productivity, costs, problems, and needs, it can plan modifications or changes to improve the business process and the business prospects. Instructions sent down the line of communication and control work their way to the workers and functions involved. At the same time the managers on each level and in each function or unit know that they are responsible for seeing that the modifications are made, and the workers under them know that they answer to their managers for their performance and compliance with instructions.

The reporting and responsibility systems are the nervous system of the business. By having the capacity to touch any operating function and direct the work of employees within any function, management can stimulate actions through the systems. It can change methods, functions, or directions on short notice and be assured that people with responsibility and accountability are looking after its interests.

Through reporting, management can constantly keep abreast of all the business pieces, and can reshuffle or deal them as necessary to maintain stability and maximize resources and opportunities.

Business Planning

Planning is conducted by management to meet a variety of business needs. It is intended to:

—Maintain operations at current levels of productivity and profitability.
—Expand productivity, sales, profits, and operations.
—Improve productivity, reduce costs, increase profitability.
—Meet competition through quality or price of services or goods.
—Identify and reach new markets for existing goods or services sold.
—Research and develop new goods or services for existing or new markets.

—Meet changes inside the operation, such as pay increases, increased costs of materials or goods, higher cost of services, increased maintenance or utility costs, or the amortization of new equipment or processes.

—Meet changes outside the business, such as higher taxes, new technology or materials, changes in consumer preferences or lifestyles, government regulations or laws, changes in the economy, or fluctuating bank interest.

—Add new equipment, or replace old equipment, to increase productivity and reduce costs or to broaden product or service lines and markets.

—Establish a better business profile for the purposes of attracting equity, getting financing, or going public.

Planning in each case requires input from all managers on all levels, as well as from the professionals or technicians listed on the functional or staffing chart. Consider how planning works and how functional and staffing charts are used.

As described before, the business is broken down into all the functions in the business process, and those functions are grouped into functional units. The staffing chart identifies the personnel required to service different functions and functional units. Managers are assigned to functions, groups of functions, or functional units, and some are often assigned to groups of functional units, called divisions.

If the business has been in operation, management has a record of its operations. It knows how many people it took to produce the work in each function, group of functions, or functional unit. It knows the amount and cost of materials and supplies required for each worker to fulfill his or her function or group of functions. It knows how many managers it took to establish a good system of control and communication. It knows what its total sales were and what its net profits were after costs. It knows its pricing structures, markets, and suppliers.

It also knows, from the reports of the managers, whether workers were working at 100% efficiency or less. It is informed about the extent of absenteeism, time lost for vacations, sickness, business interruption, holidays. It has an accurate picture of all the equipment and its condition. It knows how many salesmen it took to sell its goods and how much each can sell in a given period.

It knows its customers and how they pay—if collections are good or slow. It knows how much working capital is needed to carry operations between payments by customers. It knows how much money it may have borrowed to meet its working capital or equipment needs.

Through research and professional assistance, it can study new technology to see if it can increase productivity or reduce costs, and

Planning is putting the business pieces together to keep the operation stable and to expand.

whether it can afford to acquire such technology. It can learn of new related products or services that can be offered to old customers and new ones. It learns about new taxes, costs of electricity, rent increases, raises in union or market pay rates. It learns of rising or falling costs of raw materials or finished goods. It learns of new distributions systems, innovations in packaging, or improved design. It learns many things about what is currently going on in the economy and what is projected for the immediate future.

With such data, management can plan.

If the business wants to just maintain current levels of operation, it must identify factors that can affect costs or sales. If raw materials went up in price, then each item produced costs more. If sales dropped off, it must find out whether competition is stealing its markets, or if consumers stopped buying, or if the need for its products or services changed. It must know if governmental regulations or laws, or perhaps health services, contributed to the drop in markets. It must examine its sales policies, sales force, and distribution systems. It must devise a formula to bring sales levels up.

If worker productivity is only 50% and can be increased through better management, improved systems, new machinery, or wage incentives, then management must examine the worth of each and find ways to improve productivity. Since in these cases, increased productivity can be achieved with the same labor, unit costs go down. Sales prices can also be lowered, rendering the business more competitive.

Planning is a system of investigation and of checks and balances to achieve a purpose. Many business pieces must be fitted together in the right way to improve the operation and expand the business.

Each piece that is changed affects other pieces. For instance, if costs change, prices generally change. If production changes, costs change. It costs of labor go up, unit cost changes, and pricing must reflect the increased costs.

Without proper measuring tools it is impossible to plan for anything. The charts, the manager reports, the study of changes inside and outside the business are your basic tools for planning. They provide the data enabling management to identify its labor needs, its purchases of materials, its equipment needs, its competitive price and quality structures, and its markets.

Most important of all, these tools help management determine if it has the necessary financial resources, and if not, how much it may need to raise through borrowing, sale of equity, or other measures. It can then figure the best course to follow, based on its business potentials, its competition, and its basic resources.

Businesses must plan to survive. Planning requires periodic review and analysis. By constantly studying the business pieces and the changes inside and outside the business, a company can work constantly to hold the ground it has already won, and to expand.

Good management brings out the best in its workers.

... e welfare of its employees ... r both humane and selfish

... s responsive and interested in ... d, tend to be more productive ... business. They tend to be less ... m managers of trouble spots or ... s interruptions and damage or loss

... people, they respond to the business ... If the business premises are dirty, ... unpleasant, workers are likely to be ... be more absenteeism, sickness, and

... d regulations relating to the workplace, ... or good reasons.

... eople consider labor, health, and building ... neck, those laws are as much protection for ... employees. Nobody gains if workers suffer ... orders result from noncompliance with such

... ions cannot prevent some accidents, the com- ... ed practices reduces the danger of a business ... d with criminal negligence, or of loss of insur- ... ost businesses cannot afford to operate without ... overage.

... no comply with the law reduce the risks of injury, ... , and worker anxiety and avoid business interrup- ... nent damage or loss through fire, water damage, or ... as well as from unusual absenteeism or loss of skilled ... ployees get hurt or sick on the job. Moreover, by being ... their employees, they establish a favorable and ... ss climate. Workers will want to continue in their jobs ... e security and peace of mind found in this situation. ... rder to keep their jobs and to stay on as part of the work

Bad management brings out the worst in its workers.

Personnel Policies and Practices

In its job qualifications and description for each staff position, and its standards of performance establishing expected levels of productivity and the areas of responsibility for each staff member, management has in effect established a contract with its workers, which governs the relationships between the two parties.

Statements of personnel *policies and practices* in addition establish an understanding between management and labor of certain benefits and payments that labor will receive while employed.

For instance, when management declares in its statement of personnel policies and practices that employees are entitled to six sick days a year with pay, two weeks' vacation with pay after one year's employment, twelve paid legal holidays, overtime at 1½ times regular pay, and so on, it establishes an understanding with its workers. If employees break the agreement, they may in some cases lose their rights to benefits and payments.

The business must also establish hiring, firing, and suspension policies so that it can reward the deserving and deny rewards to the undeserving.

If a worker does not perform as "contracted," management can either dismiss the worker from employment or notify the worker that it is displeased with the performance, in which case it may give the worker a certain period of time to shape up on the job. If abuses are seriously detrimental to the business, it can simply fire the worker on the spot.

In general practice, the system of notice works better. If a worker does not perform well or causes disturbance to the business process, that worker should be notified by management that he or she is on notice. The worker should be given a period of time to improve. If no improvement follows, the worker should be dismissed. People sometimes take a little time to get adjusted in a job or to get used to new systems. On the other hand, if performance is clearly below standards, the employee may not deserve notice. After all, businesses are not welfare organizations.

Businesspeople rely on their workers to contribute to the business process and to profits. If workers perform well and the business is profitable, management can reward good workers by offering benefits and rewards. If business is bad, good workers are still entitled to basic benefits, such as holidays, vacations, and some sick days with pay. Workers should not abuse sick days, since they are provided as a gesture of goodwill to workers if they are really sick. Sick days are not vacations or holidays.

A businessperson cannot be Santa Claus.

Where unionized labor is employed, labor contracts spell out the benefits. All workers are entitled to certain benefits by law.

Under the law, they must be covered by Workmen's Compensation, Disability, Unemployment Insurance, and other protection, depending on the industry. Also, the law has established fire, health, building, and safety codes for their protection. Some workers' rights under labor laws must be posted on the business premises.

Many businesses use a probation system to evaluate workers before granting them all of the benefits.

Management may arrange with newly hired employees to have them work a period of time—two, three, or six months—before they are considered permanent employees. During this probation period such workers are not entitled to all the benefits but only to those required by law, plus vacation days or sick days and holidays. After the workers have shown that they perform well, they are made permanent employees with rights to the full benefits.

In this way management avoids the problems of hiring and firing with the complex obligations ensuing from the full benefits package.

Aside from benefits or rights established by law, all others are optional.

However, if the standard practice in an industry is to offer certain benefits or rights, or if your competition offers them, it may be difficult to attract or hold good employees if the benefits you offer are clearly inferior to those offered by others.

Mechanics of Management

At this point it will have become apparent that management encompasses many different operations and concerns in the business process. The good manager continuously uses all the tools of management to bring to bear all available resources on the business process in order to stabilize, improve, and expand it.

Independent of the size of a business, its sales, the number of employees, or its products or services, *all* businesses need good management, and good management uses the same tools.

If an operation seeks to achieve a sound business balance, management must know how one function affects another and how external influences affect the different functions and goals of the business. And if the business is to be successful, it must seek high productivity, ways to reduce costs, broader and more receptive markets, and reasonable profitability.

Only through sound knowledge and understanding of every function and of the costs associated with each staff member can management plan and expect to control its business. It must know the responsibilities and expected productivity of each staff member, the materials, goods, and supplies it needs, and their costs and quality.

The tricks of the trade are known to many competing businesses. The business with the best management has the best chance of capturing the largest piece of the pie. To hold your ground, you have to be at least as good as your competitor. Once your competitor gets a strong competitive edge, the chances of your success diminish.

Management is a skill that can be learned. It requires the discipline of attention to detail. The little facts, the little problems, the little information identified here and there in the system add up to a full picture of the total operation. No point is too small.

Businesspeople can train themselves to become good managers by proceeding systematically. Construct a functional and a staffing chart for your business. Review your employee standards and qualifications. Measure the productivity of your workers. Look at your equipment, systems, and controls.

See if you have agents throughout your operation who can responsibly report to you. Do you have a system for communication and control? How is your work environment?

Your business future is in your hands. Don't waste your chances.

3

Markets, Business Areas, and Research

Management planning identifies specific business needs: the need for capital to buy equipment, purchase materials, goods, and services; the need for labor and managers; the need for a balanced flow of supplies and services sufficient to maintain productivity at required levels and meet sales projections; the need to supply the services it offers; the need for working capital to cover the operating costs in the periods between delivery of goods or services and payment; the need for certain sales levels to maintain productivity and the flow of money into the business; the need for profit margins sufficient to provide adequate net profits after costs.

Therefore, there are three stages in the business process. First, before it can operate or meet its operational goals, the business must acquire the necessary space, facilities, equipment, machinery, labor, capital, materials and supplies, and goods and services. Second, it must do something with the materials, products, or services it buys. Third, it must sell its products or services to others.

Each business is an economic unit bridging at least two marketplaces: the one it buys from and the one it sells to.

Marketplaces are where buyers and sellers come together to trade. In most cases, businesses buy what they need in one or more different marketplaces. In economic terms, marketplaces are referred to simply as *markets*.

The markets in which a business buys its needs are called *factor markets*. The markets in which the business sells its products or services are called *product markets*.

Factor markets include all sources of capital, labor, financing, supplies and services, facilities, power, and professional services that supply the operational needs of the business. Product markets include all purchasers, users, and potential purchasers and users of the products and/or services offered for sale by the business.

In the business process, factor and product markets are directly interrelated.

In planning, management must budget its operational needs so that it will be able to run a successful and profitable business. It must purchase sufficient amounts of supplies and services so that goods for sale can be produced without interruption. It must process its goods efficiently and profitably. It must sell its products or services in sufficient volumes to offset operational costs and earn profits.

The costs of each item, such as supplies, labor, taxes, utilities, space, or fuel, are estimated by looking at past records, examining current costs, and identifying changes inside or outside the operation

*Your business bridges two or more markets. Goods and services
flow from your suppliers to your business. You do something
to them and sell your products to your customers.*

which bear on costs or may in the future bear on costs. Costs must be offset by sales volumes and pricing.

Any changes in factor markets may have a direct effect on product markets.

If a business has budgeted certain costs to enable it to operate profitably, it must seek to maintain that cost level to achieve its goals. If costs go up, profits go down unless internal adjustments are made or sales prices raised.

When prices in the factor markets, where you buy, rise, operating costs go up. Higher prices in the factor markets could result from higher costs of your suppliers, necessitating an increase in prices to you to offset their own increases in costs for rent, materials, labor, financing, equipment, and so on. Naturally, they pass their increased costs on to you. If you do not reduce operating costs to offset the increased prices in supplies or increase your sales prices to your customers, you earn less profit. Therefore, changes in the factor markets, where you buy, can directly affect your business and your pricing and services in your product markets, where you sell.

Your business must restore the proper balance between costs and revenues to insure profitability. By making adjustments in opera-

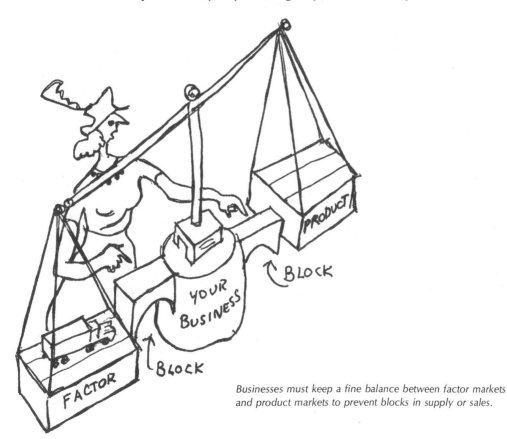

Businesses must keep a fine balance between factor markets and product markets to prevent blocks in supply or sales.

tions or pricing, product design, or quality of materials, businesses must try to insure a steady flow of supplies and sales.

If a business cannot get the supplies it needs, or get them for prices it can afford, in its factor markets, or if it must charge too much for what it sells in its product markets, then its profitability and sales may suffer. Increases in the costs of supplies, which may lead to noncompetitive sales prices, must be overcome through modifications of operations to restore the planned business balance.

A business must buy right, produce or service right, and sell right to be successful. Anything that affects the flow of supplies or services to your business or their cost, and anything that affects the flow or prices of your products and services to your customers, bears heavily on the success or failure of your operation. Whatever the reasons for changes in costs or supplies, management must constantly act to restore the balance between factor and product markets and modify operations as necessary to insure that balance.

Changes occur each day. Sometimes cost increases result from price increases in factor markets. Sometimes customer preferences and needs change, or competition affects your product markets and price structures. Supplies can dry up. Labor supply and pay scales vary. Any number of developments can temporarily throw your budget off balance.

Whatever the reasons for temporary imbalance, good management can effect changes to restore balance, to insure supply, to hold customers, to maintain its competitive capacity, to insure profits. However, first management must have a good understanding of the business process and its operating options.

The laws of supply and demand operate in factor and product markets.

Generally, when people really want a product or service, they are willing to pay a little more. The greater the demand for a product or service and the lesser the supply, the more people will pay. If demand is low and supply great, people will generally shop for the lowest price. Some examples will illustrate our point.

If fire destroyed vast tracts of industrial woodlands, trees and tree by-products would be in short supply. The number of logs going to the lumber mills and the trimmings and pulp materials going to the paper mills would decrease. The amount of lumber or paper stock produced would drop.

Those industries—such as the homebuilding industry, the paper

Sound balance is business power and success. Keep a good hold on your operations.

industry, the furniture industry, the boat industry—which use large quantities of wood or paper would be in short supply, and each would compete with the other for supplies. The prices of lumber products and paper stock in factor markets would rise, and businesses using wood or paper would incur higher costs for supplies.

To restore the business balance and to keep within price structures acceptable to their customers in their product markets, businesses would seek ways to use substitute materials, redesign their products to use less wood or wood by-products, downgrade quality, and raise their prices as possible without blocking sales to their markets. They would also seek new ways to reduce the costs of manufacturing, handling, finishing, shipping, and so on.

On the other hand, if wood and paper were in strong supply, or oversupply, builders and other user industries could use better quality wood products, design better products, and even reduce prices in their product markets.

Similarly, if the buying public became a strong market for homes, the competition among buyers would encourage homebuilders to raise their prices. If demand fell off, homebuilders would sell their houses cheaper.

Supply and demand, whether in factor markets or product markets, affect costs and sales prices.

Each business must buy what it needs in factor markets, and sell in product markets. In that sense, *each business becomes a product market to businesses which supply or service it, and a factor market to businesses it in turn supplies or services.*

The forest industries produce trees and sell logs and tree by-products to the lumber mills and paper mills. The lumber and paper mills in turn sell wood and paper to other businesses, such as lumber yards and brokers, paper dealers, and paperboard manufacturers, which in turn sell products to printers and publishers, furniture manufacturers, boat builders, homebuilders, paper-box manufacturers, and so on. These in turn sell their products to other businesses.

Most products are comprised of many smaller parts, such as various metals, woods, plastics, vegetable products, and each component part passes through many factor and product markets before the end product reaches the final customer. For instance, a piece of furniture may be made of wood, with a formica top, with metal reinforcements, with brass hardware, glass shelves, and fabric covering, and be shipped in wood-reinforced cardboard boxes.

Each material and component part flows through factor and product markets and is subject to the laws of supply and demand. Price differences for each component part of a product or service can therefore cause increases in the costs of producing or handling a product or delivering a service.

CULTIVATED
NATURAL
RESOURCES

RAW MATERIALS
(INTERMEDIATE)

INTERMEDIATE
PROCESSED GOODS

FINAL PRODUCT

FINAL PRODUCT

Management must keep track of the supply and cost of each component part of its products or services and modify its products, services, operations, or prices to maintain a sound business balance, competitiveness with other businesses, and acceptance by customers in its product markets.

Understanding the mechanics of both factor and product markets is the first step in that process. Good managers must be aware of current or projected changes in the markets. They must monitor both factor and product markets. They must devise plans to provide some degree of flexibility to meet rising costs, shortages of supplies of critical component parts, and limits of acceptance for prices in the product markets.

Factor Markets

Consider the process of converting natural resources into final products. In the long and complex process from the mining, extraction, or cultivation of natural resources, to refined raw materials, to intermediate processed or fabricated goods, to final goods or completed services, all businesses involved in the process deal in both factor and product markets.

The components of most products start in some natural form, as natural resources, which are mined, extracted, or cultivated. Metals start as mineral ores. Plastics start as petroleum or chemicals (mineral ores). Leather starts as animal hides. Wood starts as trees. Natural resources are taken from the air, land, and seas.

These resources are refined to produce basic raw materials. Raw materials are processed, combined, treated, or fabricated into many forms for many uses. *In any step between natural resources and final product or service, all products or services are intermediate products.* They are purchased for resale, further processing, or manufacturing, whereas final goods and services are purchased for final use.

A product may be a final product for one user and an intermediate product for another. Crude oil may be a final product, or it may be an intermediate product to be refined into gasoline. A log may be a final product for use in landscaping or an intermediate product to be cut into boards.

The more businesses are involved in the processing of goods or services, the more costs are added. Each business seeks to recover its costs and earn profits, and each passes those costs and profits along to purchasers in its sales prices. Prices reflect all costs and all profits.

By doing something to the product in any stage from natural resource to the final good or service, each business adds something to the product or service. That something is called *added value* since the product or service has become more valuable, or can demand more dollar value in the marketplace (either factor or product markets). Added value adds to the cost of a product or service, whether the purchaser is a business or individual consumer.

For example, trees are cultivated, then cut and trimmed. The tree farms paid for seeds, equipment, labor, land, fertilizer, pesticides, and for the cutting and trimming. They have added value by raising and cutting the trees and must recover their costs plus profits through the prices they charge the lumber mills or paper mills for the logs and trimmings. The lumber mills cut the logs into boards, and the paper mills make paper from the wood pulp and chemicals. They have added value by processing the raw materials, and they recover their costs plus profits in the prices they charge lumber yards or paper dealers for their products. The lumber yards cut wood to size or handle shipments, and paper dealers cut and package paper stock. They recover their costs and earn profits by figuring those costs in their prices to their customers, such as homebuilders, furniture manufacturers, boat builders, or, in paper, printers, newspapers, and so on. The furniture manufacturer, for example, processes and fabricates furniture and recovers its costs plus profit in the prices it charges furniture stores. And so on.

In that process, products and services move from factor to product markets, back to factor markets again, and product markets again, until the final sale. Added value operates in each case.

In any business operation, you must figure the costs of what you buy in factor markets, the costs of your operation, the costs of selling your product or service, plus your desired profit, to determine the prices of your products or services to your product markets. To be successful, a business must recover costs and earn profits.

As can be seen from these examples, businesses bridge factor and product markets and deal in both. The tree cultivators must buy land, seeds, fertilizer, machinery and equipment, hire labor, hire management, and so on. They buy their needs in factor markets. They sell the logs and trimmings to lumber and paper mills, which constitute their product markets. The mills buy the logs and trimmings from the tree cultivation farms, which constitute their factor markets.

The mills sell their products to dealers, lumber to lumber dealers or yards, and paper to paper dealers. The dealers are the mills' product market. The mills are the dealers' factor markets.

The dealers in turn sell their products to manufacturers, builders and fabricators, their product markets. Each in turn adds value, and

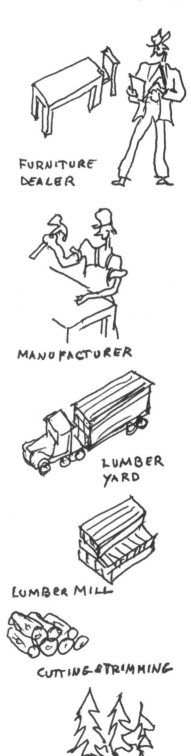

FURNITURE DEALER

MANUFACTURER

LUMBER YARD

LUMBER MILL

CUTTING & TRIMMING

TREE CULTIVATION

the cost of the final product reflects all the costs and profits of all businesses involved between the natural resources and the final product.

The more businesses involved in the process between the natural resource and the final product, the higher the cost of the final product.

In business operation and management, it is important to understand that adding to the number of businesses that get involved in the process can only lead to higher costs. Cost savings can result from less handling, fewer processes, choice of alternate or substitute materials, or from farming out work if the costs are lower than if the business did it itself. Many techniques in business relate to this concept of added value, because it is one of the keys to keeping costs down.

Factor markets must be constantly monitored to keep track of changes in prices, in products and services, in technology, in sources of supply and service.

Management must constantly seek ways to reduce costs. This not only is relevant when costs go up for some aspects of operations and balance must be restored, but also applies to opportunities to reduce costs, to become more competitive in product markets, and to enter into or develop new product markets. Supply, and the costs of supply, often determine the options which a business can exercise.

Market conditions constantly change as goods become plentiful or short in supply, new products or services are developed, lifestyles and customer preferences change, costs vary and prices fluctuate. Consumer resistance can cut sales. Shortages can cut production and sales. Increased cost of supplies can cut profits. All market conditions are interrelated and must be dealt with effectively to maintain a sound business balance.

Natural resources are limited.

There is a finite limit to natural resources. In the entire world, there is just so much iron ore, so much forest land, so much oil, gas, and copper ore. When those resources become scarcer or are in greater demand, there is that much more competition for the available supply. When competition increases the demand for the available supply, prices go up. When natural resources become short in supply or are priced out of the reach of your business, other materials must be found to replace them.

In some cases substitutes cannot be used, and as your costs rise,

WOOD = TREES

METAL = ORE

PLASTIC = OIL
BRISTLES

VARNISH = TREES

so must your prices. Where product markets demand specific products made of specific materials, costs can often be reduced through product or service modifications, such as design or size. If not, increased costs can be recovered by raising prices to your product markets.

Most products are made of component parts of materials derived from several or many different natural resources, which passed through many different intermediate processes, with added value for each process. The same holds true for materials used in services.

If a company uses natural gas for fuel and has budgeted costs for its operations based on past costs and estimated normal increases, a sudden shortage of natural gas and the resulting sharp price increase could throw the budget out of line. Furthermore, if natural-gas supplies are cut, a business may have to switch to propane gas. This would require new installations, and fuel costs would sharply rise.

If a company uses wood and leather in its products, it should project costs for those materials in its factor markets and provide for upward price trends, based on experience or economic forecasts. If a major fire in industrial woodlands or a serious reduction in the cultivation of livestock occurs, this could alter supply, increase competition, and raise costs far above budgeted estimates.

Management must break down all of its needs in order to operate and meet its planned goals. Every item it purchases in the factor markets must be identified and noted. This is true for materials as well as workforce requirements, for a business needs not only facilities, machinery, equipment, tools, and supplies, but also labor, managers, and professional services.

A business has many needs. Employee requirements can easily be identified by studying the functional and staffing charts described in Chapter 2. The other needs, such as facilities, power, fuel, equipment, space, and supplies, can be identified in the process of noting operational functions. In this way management makes sure that it has available all the materials and staff it needs to meet its production and sales goals.

Generally, increased costs of materials or labor represent the major purchases that can upset budgets. However, all costs for all items, whether they represent large or small purchases, can seriously affect budgets.

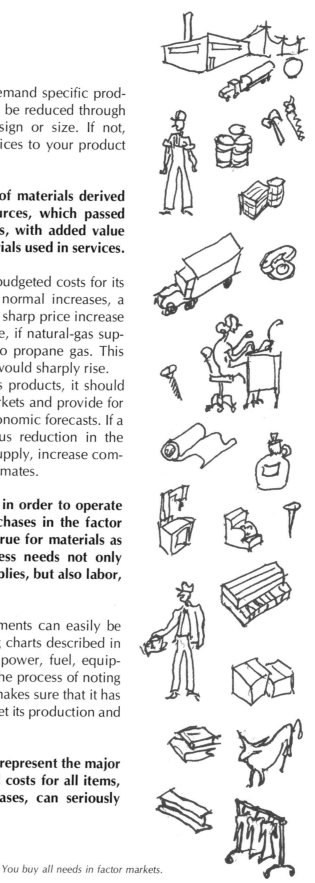

You buy all needs in factor markets.

If a furniture manufacturer must pay more for lumber supplies, a major material in that business, this would seriously throw the budget out of line. If the cost of lumber remained the same, but labor costs, the costs of power and new machinery, shipping costs, the costs of screws, glue, and hand tools rose, the effect could also add up to a serious imbalance of planned budgets. Little things, added together, add up to a lot. All costs for all purchases in factor markets are significant and must be monitored.

If an accountant raises his or her fee or your attorney charges more for preparing or checking contracts, or if the costs of labor benefits rise, your budget is affected. People necessary to your operation are operational needs and costs, like any others.

Further, management must break down the component parts of products or services it purchases to be able to cost out each component part and determine how it contributes to total cost.

PAINT BRUSH

WOOD HANDLE = 15 ¢

METAL BAND = 20 ¢

BRISTLES = 30 ¢

VARNISH = .5 ¢
_____

TOTAL COST
MATERIALS   70 ¢

If a paint brush manufacturer broke down the component parts in a paint brush, he would list: a wooden handle which was varnished; a bundle of bristles made of plastic fibers; a metal band that fastens the bristles to the wooden handle.

If the wooden handle cost 15¢, the bristles 30¢, the metal band 20¢, and the varnish 5¢, the materials needed to make the brush would cost 70¢.

If the price of wood increased, the handle might then cost 17¢. If the cost of bristles rose, they might cost 34¢. If the cost of the metal band increased, it might cost 22¢. If the cost of varnish increased, it might cost 6¢. The total cost of the materials for the brush would be 79¢.

The manufacturer has several options. One would be to raise the price of its brushes to cover increased costs. Another would be to use lighter gauge metal or a thinner band to reduce costs. Another would be to apply a thinner coat of varnish. Another would be to use another material for the band, like plastic. Another would be to reduce the quality of the brush fibers.

All such options must be evaluated against competition in product markets, customer acceptance, and utility. Clearly, one goal must be to choose modifications that least affect quality.

While the manufacturer may be able to restore the original 70¢ cost of materials through various changes, the product must stand up against the competition, must still do a reasonable job (utility), and must be accepted by customers in the product markets. Therefore, modifications to reduce costs should be selected that result in the least possible reduction of quality and utility. In this case, the bristles, which are the prime part of the brush, should be the last thing to be tampered with in cost reduction.

The answers to increased costs must be found in factor markets, in design and production methods, or in pricing in product markets.

We will deal with production and product markets later. Here we will concentrate on the relationship of markets and production.

Management must constantly monitor the costs of all purchases and labor, and of all component parts of products or services. It must keep in touch with its supply sources and seek out new ones. It must keep in touch with new technology (machines, equipment, and systems), new products and services, and, most important, with its competition.

When changes that affect costs occur in factor markets, the informed management can identify its options, find sources of supply for old or new products or services, and apply new products or services, or technology, to reduce costs and operate within planned budgets. Generally, price increases should be the last resort.

Cost increases can result from increased prices for products or services at any point between natural resources and your purchase.

If fires destroy industrial tree farms so that logs and trimmings are in short supply, the price increase of logs and trimmings, long before they are made into lumber or paper, can cause increases in prices of intermediate lumber or paper products through factor and product markets, until they reach you.

If any business in the chain of intermediate stages suffers strikes, business interruptions, increased labor costs, increased taxes, higher costs of energy or shipping, those increased costs carry through the chain in the business process. *All* businesses are affected by increased prices of needs purchased in factor markets, and all must pass those increased costs along if they cannot find acceptable ways to absorb them by reducing overall operating costs.

Each business competes with many others for supplies and services for its operational needs. That competition comes not only from the same or similar kinds of business, but from businesses in different industries selling a wide variety of products and services. All share one great similarity: They need products, services, labor, managers, and professionals for their business. They also compete for fuel, power, and financing.

Homebuilders use wood. Furniture and boat manufacturers use wood. Store or office interior contractors use wood. Building contractors use wood. Picture frame companies use wood. Many other businesses use wood in their product or service lines. All are competitors in the factor markets where they buy their wood.

If wood becomes more expensive because it is in short supply or demand for it increases sharply, all businesses that use wood are affected. If the price of trees, logs, and lumber increases, the effect is felt by all those businesses, not just by direct users of logs or lumber.

Similarly, builders use aluminum, but so do pot and pan manufacturers, foil manufacturers, and boat builders. Clothing manufacturers use leather, but they compete with automobile manufacturers, luggage manufacturers, and shoe manufacturers for this resource.

Competition is strong in factor markets. Want a piece of the pie?

Most products or services, and most component parts of a product or service, have a demand in many different industries or kinds of businesses. Very often your business competes with industrial giants for the same resources.

By virtue of their large purchases and financial resources, major purchasers often are given a ''prime'' or ''preferred'' position in factor markets. Very often their needs are met first, before remaining stocks are distributed among other purchasers. When shortages occur, the smaller purchaser generally feels the pinch first. Because of their position in markets, small businesses must be particularly alert to maintain a ''feel'' of their supplies so they can take quick steps to adjust to changing market conditions. In the business world, the small-business operators must earn success by aggressively keeping in touch with and dealing in factor markets. Very often they have to nudge their way through stronger competition to get their business needs in factor markets.

You have to work hard to get your piece of the pie, or you'll be left out.

Since major purchasers and their buying reflect the demand for particular natural resources, products, services, and component parts, their sales act as indicators of the demand for certain goods and services in factor markets.

If, for instance, automobile sales in the last quarter of the year rose by 2 million cars and increased sales were projected for the next quarter, then the demand on the available supplies of steel, aluminum, fabric, plastic, rubber, wire, glass, gasoline, oil, paint, chromium, and so on, would increase. As the demand by major purchasers accounts for more and more of the available supply, the supplies available for sale to smaller users become less, and smaller users compete more for the remaining supply.

The *increased automobile sales, announced months before supplies began to dry up for smaller users, were warnings of things to come and indicated important changes in factor market conditions.*

The data that clue businesses to coming changes in markets are called "indicators" because they indicate in advance what changes are taking place in various industries and they alert businesses to possible effects on factor and product markets and the economy as a whole.

By closely keeping track of major industries using the same (or similar) products, services, or components as your business, it is possible to be warned in advance of market changes and increased competitive demand that will affect supply and prices. The section on "indicators" later in this chapter will discuss this technique in further detail.

Even though small businesses may be tucked away on small business streets in neighborhood shopping areas or in small towns, they are all part of regional, national, and international markets by virtue of their purchasing and sales functions.

No matter where natural resources are mined, extracted, or cultivated or intermediate products and services are produced, processed, or handled, your business, as a purchaser in factor markets, contributes to the success of businesses in the chain of flow through factor and product markets in the total business process. Your purchases in New York, Atlanta, Chicago, or any smaller city or town affect businesses in France, Nigeria, Taiwan, Brazil, and every country in the world.

Of course, your prime competition is represented by businesses that offer the same products or services for sale to the same markets.

Businesses must constantly examine their immediate competition since they are both fighting for larger shares of the same product markets.

The section on "indicators" will detail ways to study your competition so that you can maintain your share of markets and find new ways to gain advantages over your competition in both factor and product markets.

Businesses must plan alternate routes to meet their needs and have plans in readiness to meet changing market conditions and prices.

Businesses must examine their products, services, and component parts and plan in advance for uses of alternate or substitute materials, modifications or redesign, or reductions in processing or handling to remain competitive without sacrificing the quality of their products and services or pricing themselves out of their product markets. Sound management constantly searches for new sources of supply

COPPER ORE MINED IN CHILE

REFINED INTO COPPER BARS IN JAPAN

ROLLED INTO COPPER SHEETS IN CALIFORNIA

MADE INTO COPPER POTS IN ILLINOIS

Sold to dealers all over the United States

and service, both for goods or services currently used and for products or services that can be employed to reduce costs.

Figure 3 summarizes the materials, products, services, and other needs businesses must buy in their factor markets. As we have seen, supplies in factor markets are not unlimited. More often than not, there is strong competition for them, and you must plan carefully to get all your needs at the right prices. If your competition buys goods or services of better or equal quality for less cost or has access to more dependable supply than your business, it is in a better position to seize business advantages and take away your customers. To

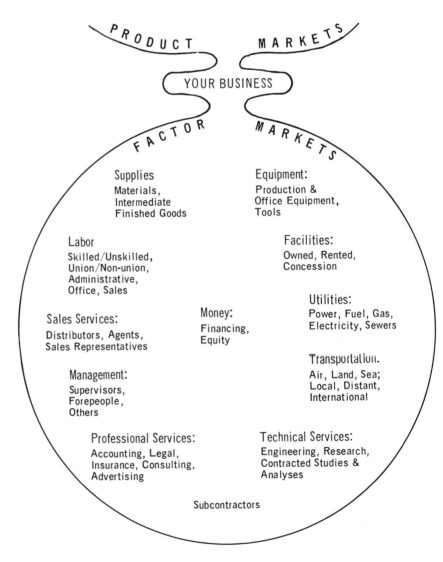

Figure 3. Your business as a bridge between factor markets and product markets.

maintain your competitiveness and protect your markets and sales, you must buy right; this is just as important as selling.

All of the operational needs of your business are purchased in factor markets. Operational needs include materials, equipment, and workforce. You compete with other businesses for the supply of those needs.

A business needs a good lawyer, a good accountant, skilled workers, efficient equipment and machinery, adequate facilities and work environments, fuel and power, and ample supply of materials, products, and services. It needs good sales representatives. At the same time, other businesses need the same things and people.

One good and skilled worker is worth ten poor workers. A good accountant can help control costs and can contribute to financial stability. A good lawyer can prevent losses and claims and effect profitable agreements and contracts. A good manager can prevent waste and loss, increase productivity, reduce costs, improve systems and controls. A good salesperson can increase sales and broaden markets. These "purchases" in factor markets are as important to business success as the supply of materials needed to produce products. Management must shop for the right people just as much as for the right materials at the right price.

All these needs demand equal attention and care if your business is to succeed.

Your Industry and Other Industries

As previously described, every business is an economic unit bridging two or more markets. All businesses are part of a chain or process of economic activity (buying and selling), which flows from the basic resources to final products.

There is a delicate interdependence among all businesses as they buy and sell in their factor and product markets. Not only are businesses dependent on each other, but they are dependent on such forces as labor, government, and a number of organizations and institutions that affect business. Therefore, it is important for each business to be clear about its place in the chain of economic activity, in its industry, and in relation to other industries and businesses. It must understand the practices and regulations governing business activity and exchange.

Some businesses share many needs and markets and are directly dependent upon each other as buyers and sellers. They can be categorized as an *industrial group.*

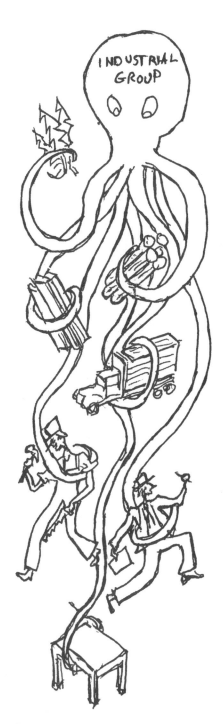

Businesses in an industrial group require similar inputs and sell closely related products or services.

The paper industry, for example, includes all establishments from pulp mills to paper and paperboard mills to manufacturers of paper products to wholesalers and distributors of paper products to retailers of paper products. These businesses, which are dependent on one another, form an industrial group.

If basic raw materials such as wood become scarce and more expensive, the whole paper industry will be affected, from the mills to the retailers. Increased costs will be passed through the chain of buying and selling, and prices will be increased accordingly. Similarly, if the demand for paper products decreases for some reason, the whole industrial group will also be affected, from the retailers and wholesalers to the mills, and prices may be lowered throughout the group.

Business success, then, is dependent not only on the management of a business, the control of its internal operations, or the conditions and acceptance in its own particular product and factor markets, but to some extent also on the supply and demand conditions faced by the industry as a whole.

Supply and demand conditions for an industrial group can be affected by many things beyond normal business operation, buying, or selling.

If, for instance, tree cultivators find that certain insects are destroying trees, they will seek pesticides to kill the insects. However, if government agencies determine that the pesticides are polluting the air or waters, they may order the tree farms to stop using them. Thus, government regulations may affect production, and less trees will be grown or be usable for lumber or wood pulp, and less supply will be available to lumber or paper mills. Competition for supplies will drive prices up, and increased costs will carry through the economic chain.

If government agencies impose certain restrictions on the trucking industry, those new rules may result in increased shipping costs, and those costs will be carried through the chain.

If government imposes embargos on certain imported goods, such as lumber or paper, the prices of domestically produced lumber or paper will rise. All businesses in the industrial group will feel the effects.

If certain institutions or organizations identify certain products or services as harmful or potentially harmful, such as tobacco, it could affect sales of products and services within the industrial group. Similarly, laws governing installment sales or advertising of products or services can effect sales, and the results would again affect the entire industrial group in some way.

Therefore, outside forces, often not directly related to the industrial group, can influence conditions within an industrial group and affect all businesses within that group. Management must monitor its industry to learn of any inside *and* outside forces that can affect its operation, purchases, sales, or manner of doing business.

Figure 4 details the major industrial group for paper and allied products. Although it primarily notes businesses within that group, it can be seen from the figure that businesses within the group deal with and affect (as suppliers) a great many different industrial groups and kinds of business operations. Here again is an illustration of the interdependence of all businesses, regardless of industrial group, in the total business process.

Figure 4 illustrates several important points. A business must know the industrial group in which it operates by virtue of the products or services it buys and sells in its factor and product markets. It must understand its position in the group to know through how many businesses the goods and services purchased in factor markets pass before they reach the business. It must know the industries and

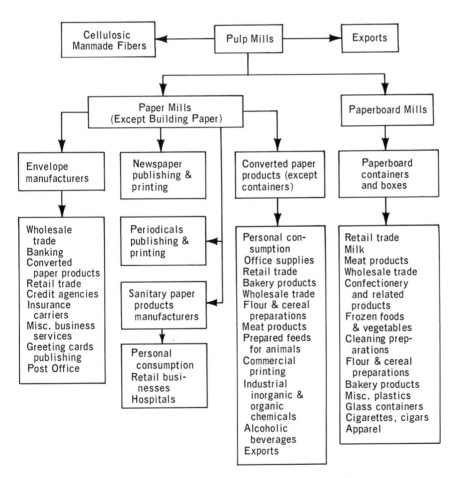

Figure 4. Paper and allied products industrial group.

kinds of businesses in the product markets of its industrial group. In short, it must know its place within the industry, as well as who sells what to whom.

First, management must decide in which industrial group the business falls. This is determined by the products and services it buys, what it does with them, and the kinds of customers to which it sells its goods.

A food processor may buy paper or paper boxes to package food items, but it is in the food processing industrial group, not the paper and allied products group. Unlike in the case of a supplier of paper products, paper is merely a component part of its operation, not its prime product or service. The prime product or service offered for sale by a business determines its industrial group.

Second, a business must identify its position in the industrial group. Does it mine, extract, or cultivate natural resources? What intermediate roles does it play in the processing chain? How many businesses are involved in the different steps in that chain before the business buys them, and how many steps are involved before the products or services the business sells become final products? This knowledge is important in monitoring factor markets.

If a paper mill buys its wood pulp materials from tree farms, and certain chemicals from refiners of natural resources, the number of businesses through which goods have passed are few. It can therefore concentrate on monitoring changes in those businesses before it in the chain. Concentration would still be directed to all other aspects of the industrial group and outside forces, but its factor markets (suppliers) and costs of supplies would be the prime concern.

At the same time, the business must look down the chain at all the subsequent users of its products or services to determine the number of businesses involved in the process and the added value which would be accrued before the final product is put on the market. If its costs should increase because of increased costs of its purchases in its factor markets, then costs may increase down the chain unless the business can make modifications to restore the balance in other ways.

Sometimes cost increases early in the process determine customer acceptance of final products or services. If an automobile, for example, finally sold for $4,000, and passed-along costs down the chain caused its price to increase to $5,000, would final customers be willing to pay that price, or would sales drop?

If a steel mill, which buys ore from mines, finds the cost of ore sharply increased and cannot modify operations to absorb the increase, it may raise prices on the steel products it sells. But it must

Where is your business within your industrial group?

43

consider how that increase, passed down the line, would affect the prices of final products made from steel. If certain products made from steel would be priced too high in markets, customers may seek substitute products or resist purchasing, and sales may drop. If sales drop, then the entire industrial group will feel the effects. The fabricators and manufacturers of products using steel will feel it. The wholesalers of steel will feel it. The mills will feel it. The mines will feel it.

Businesses must know their place in industrial groups and constantly look backward and forward along the chain. This is an essential function of business management. Businesses must also constantly study their product markets, whether or not they fall into the same industrial group.

From our chart of the paper and allied products industrial group, it can be seen that users of paper products—as component parts of other products or services or as final products used in operations—represent members of many industrial groups. Paper is used in the food processing industrial group, the medical supply group, the insurance group, the finance and banking group, and many others.

If the costs of paper products increase at any point in the business process, causing final products to rise in price, the increased costs of component parts or operational materials made of paper will rise in cost. Again, users in product markets, regardless of industry, may seek substitute materials or modifications to offset costs, or final customers may resist the purchase of products made by your customers. Reduced sales of paper products in any product market, as final or intermediate goods, can affect the entire paper and allied products industrial group.

If certain product markets that are large users of paper products suffer economic declines and their sales drop off, so does their demand for paper products. A sudden drop in food processing, which uses paper packaging, would affect sales of paper products, the available supply of paper products, and all businesses involved in the paper and allied products group.

Once management determines its position within its industry, it can accurately separate its factor and product markets. It can determine on whom the business depends for materials, products, and supplies. It can determine how many suppliers are available to it, how many businesses there are at the preceding level of the industrial structure, and what are its product markets. It can determine the number of businesses involved between it and the final products, and the markets and potentials for those products. The importance of this cannot be overestimated.

If, for example, there is a reduction in output at the paper mills, the whole industry will be affected. If the reduction of supply is at the

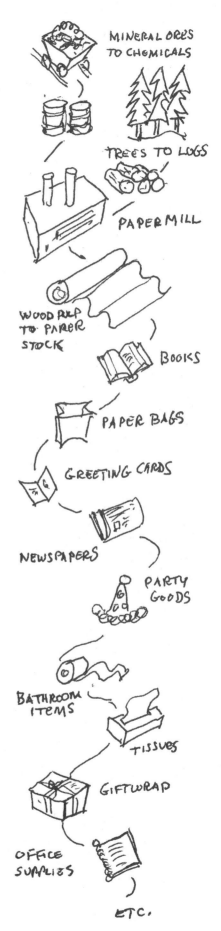

paperboard manufacturer's level, the effect will be restricted primarily to manufacturers of paperboard containers and their product markets (see Figure 4). Knowing the position of your business within the industry allows management to react to changes in the various sectors of the industry.

Also, as an integral part of an industry, each business in an industrial group is affected by the trends in its industry. Management must be aware of new products, new technology, and new markets that affect the industry and, therefore, the business.

Management must also keep abreast of new laws and regulations that affect the industry in some way or another. Many businesses and industries are associated with organizations that monitor federal, state, or local legislation and regulations affecting individual businesses or industries on different levels.

In most fields, there are trade and industrial publications available to businesspeople. Newspapers and news magazines have economic and financial sections that provide economic forecasts and reviews of business conditions for particular industries and markets. Also, libraries have great numbers of books dealing with specific kinds of businesses, industries, and industrial analyses and forecasts.

The section on research at the end of this chapter will identify some sources of relevant business data.

Another point that must be appreciated is that industries grow at different rates, depending on a number of conditions.

A "mature" industry like the automobile industry will grow at a fairly constant rate over the years, depending on consumer and commercial demand. The place of the automobile has been established in the society and the economy. On the other hand, an industry in its infancy, like the solar-energy industry, can grow very fast if certain technological and cost factors can be improved.

Management must be familiar with its industry and its growth rate in the past, its potentials for growth, and its limitations. As an integral part of an industry, your business will be affected by the overall rate of growth of the industry.

If your industry is expanding rapidly, opportunities exist for your business to share in new product markets and in the development of new products or services to meet new demands. You will still have to concentrate on competitive capacities and a balanced business operation, and on the development or acquisition of new products or services, expansion of existing product and service lines, increased supply and supply sources, stepped-up production capacities, and on the resources, whether material, human, or financial, to carry your business through its expansion period.

If your industry is stable or growing at a slow rate, the focus must be on competitiveness and tight management controls to insure that purchases, production, sales, and overall costs and pricing keep your operation in balance. Management must seek ways to reduce costs, increase competitiveness, and seize larger shares of existing product markets.

It takes time to research and analyze data, to develop sound business plans and implement them. By keeping alert to early warnings of significant changes in your industry, whether for better or worse, management can prepare for the impact of those changes on the business. It can modify operations as needed to insure a healthy balance in the periods of change. It also needs time to arrange for the resources it will require in order to expand or seize opportunities.

When an industry is growing, all the businesses in that industry seek ways to competitively grab larger product markets and sales or to modify or develop products and services to meet expanding demand. They also compete for available supplies in factor markets and seek to identify new sources of supply to meet their needs. While opportunities increase when an industry is growing, so does competition for supplies, customers, labor, and financing.

A business must know when and how to wind up or down.

Regional and Local Economic Areas

As economic units, all businesses are part of economic areas and contribute directly and indirectly to the local region in which they are located, to the economic areas in which they buy and sell, and to the larger economic areas involved in various ways as factor or product markets in the overall business process.

Wind up? Wind down? How? When? Where?

A business may be located in a small town in the state of Massachusetts. It buys its facilities, its labor, its fuel and power, and many of its supplies in local factor markets. In these ways it contributes to the local economy as employer, purchaser, taxpayer, and supplier of products or services to local markets. The business therefore is an integral part of that local economy or business community and contributes to its growth and well-being.

The same business may deal in factor markets in New York State, Connecticut, Pennsylvania, and New Jersey. It may sell to product markets in all of New England, Chicago, Cleveland, and Columbus.

By buying in factor markets, and selling to product markets, in other states, the business contributes to the economic activity in those states. In particular, through its purchases in factor markets in other states it encourages business development in those states and helps increase employment, trade, and production, resulting in higher tax revenues, more consumer purchases, more private and public building, and so on.

But just as a business has an impact on the economic activity in its business areas, so do the areas affect the business through laws, regulations, and availability of such resources as labor, transportation, necessary public services, and energy, which are essential to the majority of businesses in the area, regardless of the industry or type of business. Management must keep informed of local and regional changes in its business areas and anticipate their effects on the business.

Business is involved with specific geographical areas in three ways. First, its operations are affected by the tax structure, labor supply, and availability of energy, transportation, and other public services in the area where its facilities are located. Second, it is vulnerable to changes in the areas where it buys its supplies (that is, where its factor markets are located). Third, its sales are influenced by the socioeconomic and regulatory environment in the areas where it sells its goods (that is, where its product markets are located). Each area will have its own social, economic, and demographic characteristics. Changes in those characteristics can affect the business to a lesser or greater degree.

If a local, state, or federal agency changes rules or regulations governing certain business activities, this can affect your markets, even if those laws apply to an area far removed from your facility. For instance, if you sell certain products in California and Ohio and the governmental agencies institute controls affecting the sale of your products, your product markets in those states are affected. If suppliers in factor markets in other states face legislation regulating the use or distribution of power supply, they may be forced to cut

Management must keep abreast of changes in its business areas.

production or raise costs to meet new conditions. Those changes will affect your business.

If competition for skilled labor in the area in which your suppliers operate should increase, they may develop labor shortages, be forced to cut back production, and interrupt your supply. If a railroad line suspends operations, it may force a supplier far away to ship by truck and raise prices to you.

Management must keep in close touch with its business areas, just as it must keep informed about its factor and product markets and the industrial groups in which it falls or which affect its product markets.

Product Markets

A business buys its factor inputs in its factor markets and does something to them to make them into its products and services. It seeks to sell those products and services in its product markets. But before it can do this, it must know which buyers are in its product markets and must have an estimate of the item or dollar volumes they can purchase from it.

In planning to sell to product markets, management must be aware of the fact that it may not be beneficial to the business to sell to all of the potential buyers demanding the products or services of the business.

Many businesses or consumers (individuals, governments, agencies, and various institutions) that use the types of products or services your business offers for sale may not be the best buyers for your goods. They may not meet your conditions of sale—such as your sales prices and terms or minimum-purchase stipulations—or the credit rating you demand of your customers.

Selling is a mutually beneficial transaction. It must be advantageous and profitable to all parties, buyers and sellers.

You must know your actual product markets and your sales potentials.

If a sale is not good for your business or a purchase is not beneficial to your customers, then that transaction should not be made. If a customer buys your products or services but cannot pay for them or takes too long to pay, that customer may not be good for your business. If a customer is too small a user of your products and services, it may not pay to supply that customer. Similarly, if the customer is a large user but gets discounts from other suppliers that you cannot match, it is not a good customer for your business.

In theory your product markets include all customers that purchase, use, or consume your kind of products or services, are located in your business areas, and can be served by your business. In fact, however, your real product markets include only those customers who are actually interested in buying your products or services and are willing and able to pay for them and meet your sales terms and conditions. Also, only those businesses in your operating or business areas to which it is profitable and efficient to sell can be included in your actual product markets.

In business, a sale must be profitable to your operation. If it is not profitable, it is a loss. The purpose of business operation is not merely to cover costs but also to earn a profit above costs. Only customers able to contribute by their purchases to your business success are good for your business.

If a customer cannot pay for purchases, he will only cause a loss to your operation. If he cannot pay you within the time limit you consider necessary to insure a sound cash flow, then he is also bad for your business. If he is not really interested in buying your goods or services or wants discounts or special treatment you cannot provide, he is not good for your business.

Buyers who do not now buy from your business but can meet the above conditions are potential customers and can be included in your actual product markets, whether they are new or established businesses or are currently served by your competition.

Your must estimate the size of your actual product markets and their volume (quantity they purchase) and dollar potentials so that you can purchase in your factor markets the supplies you need to profitably fill the purchase orders from your product markets. You must also meet the levels of production necessary to recover costs and earn profits.

The methods and techniques used for researching product markets and estimating their needs and volumes of purchases and dollar value are part of the *marketing function,* which will be discussed in the next chapter.

In the following, both actual and potential product markets will simply be called "product markets." They will be understood to

Examine your product markets and choose only those customers that are good for your business.

49

mean those consumers, businesses, institutions, or governmental agencies that are interested in buying products and services like the ones your business sells, are willing and able to pay for them, and can meet your sales terms and conditions. Those buyers may be businesses in your own industrial group or in other groups, or consumers (individuals), institutions, and agencies located in the areas where you sell your products or services.

For example, a business selling paper products can sell its goods to businesses engaged in manufacturing, retail, wholesale, distribution, supply, service, or professional fields, within any industrial group and located anywhere in the world, as well as to consumers or other buyers.

Product markets can cut across industrial groupings and cover businesses of every size and kind. They can include all businesses, buyers, or consumers in a given category or just certain ones. For instance, all consumers may be covered, or only those of particular age, sex, income group, taste, interests, or combinations of these characteristics. They may be located in a single area or in several local, regional, national, and international business areas.

The final consideration in including a buyer in your product markets is whether that buyer can meet your conditions of sale and is willing and able to buy from you and pay for the purchase, and whether the sale is good for your business.

A product market, as we said, must be large enough to enable you to sell enough products and services at your prices so that your business can recover the costs of operations and supplies and earn a profit over and above all costs.

In some businesses, a small number of customers is sufficient to insure a profit; in others, many customers are needed. The amounts that each customer can buy, the prices you charge, and the sales volume your business needs to recover costs and earn profits determine your goals (target sales, number and kind of customer, and so on) in your product markets.

Each business must capture a share of product markets sufficient to enable it to recover all costs and earn profits. Once that share has been obtained, businesses may seek to increase their market shares further. Often that can be done through improved sales techniques and marketing, improved quality and design, better pricing, and in many other ways, such as advertising or packaging. A number of those techniques will be discussed later.

Your customers and sales, at your prices, must be heavy enough to overcome all costs and leave profits.

Therefore, identified product markets must be of sufficient size to

enable your business to capture its share of the market, and that share must be large enough to meet your business needs.

For instance, a business selling accounting supplies may sell its products to retailers, wholesalers, manufacturers, and distributors in different industrial groups. Those buyers can be large or small, in small towns or big cities, near or far away, and in all types of businesses. The total sales to all these customers must generate sufficient dollar sales and revenues to enable the business to recover all costs and earn a profit.

The products and services of any one business may be intermediate goods to some customers and final products to others.

A paper dealer may sell packaged paper to a stationery store, which merely stocks it on its shelves and sells it as is to its customers.

The dealer may sell paper products to printers, which cut it into various sizes, print on it, and sell it as books, magazines, advertising posters, greeting cards, and so on. The paper may also be sold to a manufacturer of paper bags, which cuts, pastes, and assembles the paper into bags of all kinds and sizes.

Product markets include all actual customers that can use the products or services of the business, whether they use them as you deliver them, in finished states, or as intermediate products (component parts of products or services) that they may process, handle, manufacture, fabricate, or in some form offer to their product markets. You are a factor market to them.

One customer may use paper to package food products that it manufactures, another, to manufacture greeting cards or prints of photographs or famous paintings. Still another may use it to make party favors, paper hats, and cups.

Your business must identify all kinds of buyers that use your products or services as finished goods or as intermediate goods or services. It must then select those buyers which qualify for inclusion in your actual product market.

Buyers need not be businesses. They can be government agencies, hospitals, schools and colleges, medical associations, prisons, and museums. All kinds of users must be identified. Once a business has identified all the actual or potential customers for its products or services, it can determine whether or not the market size is sufficient to give the business an adequate share of the total sales, after allowing for the share that will be taken by competitors.

The different kinds of users, such as businesses, individuals, agencies, institutions, or schools, that qualify to be included in your product market represent the *market composition* of your product market. The money spent for purchases in your product area is the *buying power* of your product market. Different kinds of users of your products or services in the market composition of your product markets may buy different amounts at different times. The buying power of your product market is the total of all purchases by all kinds of users, large and small, in the market composition of your product market.

For example, a supplier of leather products may have such customers in its product market as furniture manufacturers, belt makers, shoe manufacturers, luggage manufacturers, wallet manufacturers, clothing manufacturers, and pocketbook manufacturers. All the different kinds of customers make up the market composition of the product market. The amount of money that all those kinds of businesses spend or can spend for purchases of leather products is the buying power of that product market.

By studying the market composition of your product markets, your business can tell which kinds of users spend more or less for purchases of products or services like yours. You then can tell what products or services are in greatest demand by your different kinds of customers, and which products and services should be produced, processed, handled, or fabricated by your business to meet its customers' needs.

Also, analyzing the market composition of your product markets gives you a picture of the strengths and weaknesses of your business. If, in the example above, the shoe manufacturers and luggage manufacturers began to purchase less from your business, you could attempt to increase sales to other kinds of businesses in your market composition. Your business should buy the products and services it needs in its factor markets according to the needs and purchases of different users in its product market.

By knowing its market composition in product markets, a business can study trends in different industries and forecast the demand for its products and services by the different kinds of customers in the product market, whether businesses, individuals, agencies, or institutions.

If the leather dealer learns that the forecast of luggage sales for next year is poor, it knows in advance that it must buy or prepare fewer products or services to meet the needs of luggage manufacturers. It may learn that the apparel industry forecasts a good year for leather clothing. The business can buy or prepare more of its products or services to meet the expected increased demand by the apparel industry. If one kind of customer buys less, the business must sell more to another kind of customer to maintain business balance. By

The size of your product markets and their demand for your products and services must meet your business needs.

studying market composition, a business gets clues to changes in demand and can take steps to restore its sales levels and business balance.

The business can also seek new users of its products or services to replace customers that are buying less. Therefore, as conditions change, businesses change and expand their market composition and product markets.

Businesses seek to maintain a constant demand for their products or services to insure business balance.

Market demand is a measure of the amount of your products and services the buyers in your product markets want to buy, or can buy, at your sales prices. As your (or your competitors') prices change, the demand for your goods may increase or decrease.

Market composition together with the market buying power describes the strength of the demand by different kinds of businesses in your product markets and gives you an indication of the amount of money that buyers of all kinds have allocated, or have available, for purchasing the kind of products or services your business sells. If research shows that a drop in sales is to be expected for particular segments of the product market, the business may switch the emphasis in its buying in factor markets, or in its production, to supply more to strong markets and less to weak ones. In this way the business plans ahead to reach and sell to strong markets so as to overcome reductions in purchases by weak markets.

Product markets can change as your or your customers' business operations change.

If you change your sales terms and conditions, many buyers that you couldn't serve before may now be acceptable as customers. If, for instance, you insisted on payment in 30 days from delivery, many customers may have been unable to meet your conditions, and you could not serve them. If you accepted payment in 60 or 90 days, many of them would probably qualify as customers and become part of your actual product markets. If you accepted smaller purchases, the same may happen. In many ways, by changing policy, a business can increase its product markets. However, those changes must be good for the business, or they serve no purpose.

The market composition can change as a business directs its operations toward the strengths in its product markets, identifies and enters into new product markets, or offers new products or services.

In the course of doing business, an organization may discover that certain parts of its product markets have become too poor in demand

and buying power to warrant attention. Other parts of its product markets may show unusual strength, demand, and buying power. New product markets may open up for its products or services, or for new products or services. Always moving toward strengths in its markets, the business may replace some poor customers with larger or new customers, and over a period of time its market composition will change in response to market demand and market buying power. That is how it should be. A business must gravitate to sales and customers that do the most for the business and keep it balanced and expanding.

The market demand and market buying power of the different kinds of buyers in your market composition depend on conditions that increase or decrease the money available to them to buy your products or services.

Businesses, individuals, government agencies, institutions depend on different sources for their money. Individual consumers depend on income from wages, salaries, bank interest, investments to derive the money they need to buy products and services. Private businesses depend on revenues from the sale of their products or services. Government agencies depend on taxes and other sources of revenue to purchase their needs. Institutions and associations may depend on memberships, donations, grants, and funded contracts to get the money they need to buy what they need.

By knowing the sources of money of the many kinds of buyers in your market composition, it is possible to estimate whether they will have more or less money available to them to purchase products and services like yours. You can estimate the demand and buying power of each kind of buyer and for the product market as a whole.

Wanting or needing products or services is not enough. A buyer needs the money to pay for them. If the money available to your product markets decreases, the buying power and consequently the demand will decrease. If the supply of money increases, buying power and demand may increase. Therefore, businesses must study their product markets and their composition and buying power in order to estimate the demand for their products or services and plan their purchasing and production.

   If an industrial group within your product markets suffers a strike and its production stops, its demand and representative buying power drops. If a business or industrial group in your product markets sells goods or services that are in less demand or out of style, its potential to buy decreases. If economic conditions in the business areas of your

Keep track of the conditions in your markets; they affect your business.

product markets change for the worse, your customers may not have money to buy your products or services. A great many things that affect you may happen to your product markets, including government regulations or new laws which may force your customers to cut purchases.

If you sell directly to consumers employed mostly in the same industry and that industry suffers a slowdown in sales, causing it to lay off employees, some of your customers may lose their jobs. That would reduce their buying power and their demand for your products or services.

If you sell products or services to the automobile industry and hear that there will be a strike or that car sales are expected to drop off next year, or that car prices are going to increase, then you can translate that information into its possible effects on your sales and operations.

If you hear that a major company has closed its plant in a certain town and that unemployment in that town will be unusually high, you can project that businesses in that town will have slow sales and that the demand and buying power of your customers in that town will decrease.

Whatever affects your product markets affects your business. By studying your market composition, you can identify the potential trouble spots, the strengths and weaknesses. You must modify your operations and direct your business toward its areas of strength.

Knowing in advance about strengths and weaknesses in product markets reduces costs and losses.

If you know in advance that certain users of your products or services will have less demand and buying power, you can modify your purchases in factor markets, your production, your inventory, and so on, to meet new conditions and maintain a healthy business balance. You can seek new customers to make up for the slack or try to increase sales to other customers. You can modify your product or service lines. You can add new products and services to attract new product markets.

If you wake up too late, you may be unable to make the necessary modifications and may suffer losses, severe cuts in sales and production, and shortages of working capital.

A business cannot afford to wake up too late. Most businesses are not strong enough to take the severe shock of sharply reduced sales.

Product markets are also defined by the *market areas* and *market levels* that the business sells to.

Market areas generally refer to a grouping of customers in product

If you do not watch your markets and make changes when necessary, you may wake up to find that your sales are dried up and your revenues gone.

markets which share certain characteristics and, for ease of planning or supply, are given attention as a group rather than as individuals.

A paper supplier, for instance, may consider all retail users as one market area, all customers in manufacturing as another, and all users of certain kinds of paper products, such as paper bags, as a third. Market areas may group together all customers in the same kind of business or in a certain geographical area.

A business may group into a market area all government agencies or schools it sells to. On the other hand, it may make two market areas of schools: one, high schools; the other, elementary schools. It may group individual consumers it sells to by age, sex, income, education, height, weight, family size, or place of residence. It may group them as homeowners, apartment dwellers, laborers, professionals, government workers. Also, market areas may be made up of buyers with several characteristics, like businesswomen over forty years of age, or laborers with college education.

Grouping into market areas is a means to plan for the supply and service of buyers which share certain characteristics and needs.

Not only are customers grouped into market areas because of some characteristics they share, they are also grouped into market levels. Market levels describe particular levels of pricing, quality, size, style, or other product or service characteristics.

For example, let us assume that in a certain business area of an office equipment manufacturer, its product market (buyers of office equipment) has an actual buying power of $10 million a year for office equipment. Half of all purchases are for typewriters, so this market area (typewriters) accounts for $5 million a year. $3 million of that money is spent for high-priced typewriters, and $2 million for low-priced models. There are two market levels: one for high-priced and one for low-priced typewriters.

If your business sells $1 million worth of high-priced typewriters to that business area, in that product market, then it has captured one-third of the total market level, or one-fifth of the total market area, or one-tenth of the total product market.

Products and services with varied characteristics can have different markets. Within the men's apparel product market, for example, higher-priced men's suits (which belong in the product area of men's suits) have a somewhat different market (group of buyers and potential buyers), or market level, than much lower-priced suits. Similarly, a seller of a two-seat sports coupe would be selling to a different product area than a seller of a large family-sized sedan. While both sellers operate in the automobile product markets, their product areas (sports cars versus family-sized cars) are different, and their market levels could also be different, depending on the prices of the cars and other terms and conditions.

To recapitulate, the term *product market* refers to those buyers that are willing and able to pay for products and services, are interested in buying them, and can meet your sales terms and conditions. *Market areas* are those groupings within product markets which share certain characteristics. Those characteristics may be specific products or services (such as suits, cars, houses, lumber, plywood, nails, or leather), geographical areas, kinds of businesses (such as retail, wholesale, or supply), or others. *Market levels* refers to products or services that have similar characteristics but vary in price, quality, size, or style.

As the characteristics of particular products and services become more similar, market areas and levels may overlap and merge into broader levels.

Because of cost increases in production, products in lower market levels sometimes approximate in price the lower end of a higher market level. Consider two levels of men's suits, one selling from $150 to $200, the other from $75 to $100. If the lower-level suits are raised in price to the $125 to $175 range, there develops an overlap of products on two levels. If the overlap is extensive, the two levels may become one larger level. Whereas each had its own market (buyers) before, they now share the same market—the total from the two previous levels.

As suppliers of products and services sell to market areas with overlapping market levels, the competition among suppliers increases.

In our example, whereas originally one manufacturer supplied the suits in the $150 to $200 range and another those in the $75 to $100 range, they now may both supply suits selling to a new market level of $125 to $200. This means that although their markets in one sense expanded, their competition also increased, especially for the middle range, suits selling from $150 to $175.

In practice, all businesses selling to the same product markets are to some extent in competition with one another, independent of market levels.

Buyers of goods or products can choose to buy goods and services at different levels as they see fit. Therefore, by merely being available,

Within the homebuilding industry, a $70,000 house will fall into a high market level of the one-family-home market area, whereas a $35,000 house would fall into a lower market level in the same product area. A $50,000 one-family home, on the other hand, may attract customers willing to consider both $70,000 and $35,000 homes: it overlaps the two market levels.

57

goods and services on all levels may appeal to the same product markets at different times to fit different needs.

A customer of yours may have successfully operated as a retailer of fine men's suits selling for $150 to $200. If the business area in which the retailer operates suddenly declined and its customers could not afford expensive suits, the company may decide to purchase suits that can be sold for $75 to $100. Things change.

You have competitors in all markets. If you seek to expand your business and increase sales, you must either add customers by enlarging your product market or seize a larger share of the existing market. If the demand and buying power of the total market increases and your sales remain the same, it means that your share of the market has decreased.

The more competitors in product markets, the more difficult it is for a business to capture a large market share. To compete, the business must look at the quality of its product and services, its prices, its sales terms and conditions, its delivery, and its relationship with customers in product markets, market and product areas, and market levels.

The first thing a business must know is what it offers as products and services, what buyers need those products and services, what their demand and buying power are, what they are willing to pay for those products and services, and what sales terms and conditions are acceptable to them. Next, it must know the market composition of its identified product markets and understand what affects the various customers' potential to buy. It must group customers into market areas and market levels for better monitoring and service.

It must know its competitors and what they offer their customers. It must compare the prices and quality of goods and services sold by the competition and compare them to its own. It must know the competition's terms and conditions of sale.

Only when it has all these facts can management determine courses of policy or action that are beneficial to the business, that can assure the business of sufficient markets to enable it to operate successfully.

When a business knows its market composition and the potentials and problems of buyers in that composition, it can determine its own potentials.

If a business is too heavily tied to the success or failure of one kind of

BOAT BUILDER

HOME BUILDER

FURNITURE MANUFACTURER

BOX MANUFACTURER

Diversification can build security into your business. For instance, if a lumber dealer diversifies its markets, decline in one market may be absorbed by higher sales in another market.

user of its products or services, drops in purchases by those users may so seriously upset the balance that the business cannot recover. It is safer for businesses to have product markets that are diversified so that the decline of any one group of buyers will not seriously affect operations and profitability. Dependence on one or a few markets (whether groups or individual purchasers) is not always a good business practice, even if at the moment your business operates profitably and at full capacity. Management must build in safeguards.

Diversification of customers can be a business safeguard.

If a lumber dealer sells to the homebuilding industry alone and the rate of new houses being built drops sharply, the dealer may lose his sales, and in effect the business. If that dealer also sold to the boat, furniture, and box industries, the loss of business from any one area would be only a partial loss of total sales. There is safety in numbers.

Product markets are affected by changes in factor markets.

If new products or services are developed or new materials introduced, or if new technology is developed, they may affect customer acceptance of your products and services and therefore your sales and sales potentials. Customers may want the "new" or "improved" model, plastic products, products of different design or color, or products reflecting the latest in electronic technology. If you cannot meet the changing demands for goods or services in your product markets, your competition will.

Also, changes in costs of supplies in your factor markets may cause you to raise prices of your products and services. In doing this, you may price yourself out of your markets. Alternatively, shortages of supplies that you must buy in your factor markets may cause you to cut production and sales.

Management must constantly monitor factor markets to discover what changes that may affect sales and customer acceptance are taking place. At the same time, it must monitor product markets to identify changes in customer needs or preferences. *The business environment is constantly changing and requires continuous monitoring.*

Factor and product markets interact, and conditions in those markets change constantly. Most often your business did not cause those changes or can do nothing to stop them. All you can do is react to them in sound business ways.

If shortages of supply, labor problems, increasing costs, or heavy demand affect factor markets, your supply, your costs, and your ability to meet your sales and maintain your prices and sales terms are affected. Very often your competitive capacity also suffers. Your product markets will feel the effects, too. They may get less supply, poorer service, reduced quality, and may have to pay more for their needs.

If product markets resist the purchase of certain goods or services, if styles and preferences change and your customers reject your products or services or prefer products using new materials, your business is affected—and so are your factor markets. If product markets buy less, less has to be purchased from businesses in factor markets. If demand is high in product markets, then demand is greater in factor markets and prices may rise with costs. If styles and preferences change in product markets, then the amount and kinds of products and services purchased in factor markets may change.

Businesses in other industrial groups purchase the same kinds of products and services in factor markets as your business. If the demand for those products and services by others is strong and competition for supply is high, then the supply of products and services your business buys may be reduced, and prices may rise. Such shortages are sure to have an impact on your sales.

In many cases, changes are caused by events outside your business, such as strikes, government regulations, new taxes, business interruptions, shortages of natural resources or intermediate goods. Figure 5 illustrates some of the interactions between factor and product markets. As indicated in the figure, your business lies in between these markets and acts as a bridge between them. When changes occur in either factor or product markets, you must respond to them and modify your operations to restore a healthy business balance.

Indicators

For a business to operate successfully, its management must keep in touch with its factor and product markets, the factor and product markets of its own industrial group and other groups, the product markets of its customers, its competition, the economy, market demand and buying power, laws and regulations, its business areas, new technology, new products or services, new materials, the labor supply, and all costs of operations.

Changes in any of the above could affect your business, its operations, its supply, its sales and profits. It is important for management to know what is going on now and what can be expected in the future so that it can plan ahead to insure a sound business balance and prepare for changes that may affect the business.

To make broad in-depth studies of all areas in the business

process on a regular basis would take too much time and effort. Management must find quick and simple ways to get its important information, and to get it in a simple and brief form.

Each year tons of magazines, books, papers, and reports are published by government agencies, private research groups, trade associations, trade journals and papers, industry groups, manufacturers and suppliers. It would be impossible for management to study all of the material published.

However, there are a small number of sources in which important data and information can be found, and in brief and concise form. These data represent the important facts and figures derived from the research and analyses published elsewhere in full form.

Those brief reports, which condense the pertinent data, often in numerical form, can supply the information you need. They are called "indicators" because they indicate the changes and trends in

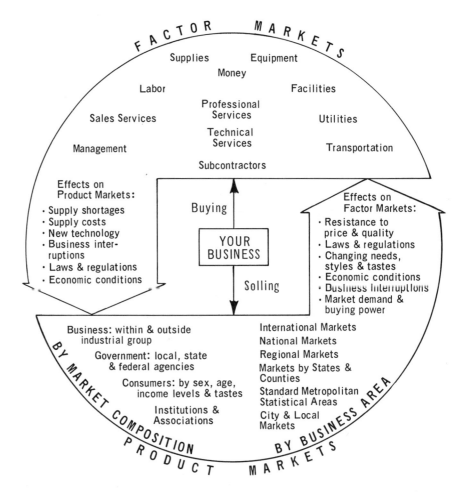

Figure 5. Interactions between factor markets and product markets.

all the areas of concern to management, thereby making it easy for management to collect the facts it needs to manage well and plan ahead.

Indicators provide a quick picture and analysis of the conditions, changes, and trends that bear on the successful and profitable operation of a business, now and in the future.

Indicators used by government agencies, private-industry economists, and professionals in other fields are based on *indices* for specific business areas, product markets, or economic areas; that is, they compare figures for one year (the *base year*) with those for one or more other years. In this way, they translate changes in the rate of unemployment, in prices, in supply, or in buying patterns and preferences into trends. Such comparisons enable analysts to tell in which year observed changes occurred and what kinds of changes can be expected for future years.

Major corporations and government agencies generally use complex techniques and large amounts of data and indices to measure many different business or operational conditions. The complexity of their operations and the diversity of their markets or their products and services necessitate a complex and deep study. By contrast, the indicators needed by small-business managements to make sound business decisions in operations and planning are less complex and often much easier to collect and analyze.

For instance, a manufacturer of plumbing supplies and parts may be concerned with the price of copper, cast iron, and aluminum—the prime metals used in plumbing supplies. If changes in factor markets or product markets threaten to affect the supply or price of those materials, the costs of purchases by the manufacturer may change, or the prices it charges its customers may have to be changed to meet competition.

Indicators are signs that help you keep your business from getting into trouble.

If, in the course of studying the relevant indicators, that same manufacturer found that the housing and homebuilding industries expected a good year because housing starts were expected to rise sharply, management would know that the demand for plumbing supplies in its product market was about to increase, along with the product market's buying power.

The manufacturer could then study its market composition and select those customers that are engaged in building for a concentrated sales effort, or it could seek new customers in the building industry. A business must go where the strengths can be found.

Whereas big business may have to study all kinds of complex statistical data and conduct involved mathematical analyses, small business can use readily available publications put out by government, trade and industry associations, and private business publishers to find its needed data. Most often, the indicators needed by small business can be found in simple form.

Suppose that you sell products to a diversified product market including the electronics industry, in particular, the television market area, and that your product is used for the specific product area of color television sets. If a market indicator researched by an electronics industry association or a government agency stated that the sales of color television sets are expected to increase from 5 million sets this year to 10 million sets next year, this would tell you that chances are excellent for your business to increase its sales to the electronics industry. On the other hand, if the indicator showed that the number of sets to be sold next year will be far smaller than this year, you would know that your sales to the electronics industry may drop in the coming year.

A simple indicator of this kind, documented by facts from respected sources, could help you plan ahead for production and sales and insure your supply in factor markets.

To stay with our example, suppose your product is made of metal. If you learn from the newspapers that the price of the metal you use has been rising in price over a long period of time, you would naturally be concerned about its cost to you now and in the future. If other sources of data indicated that the price will continue to rise until it is almost 50 percent higher than what you have to pay now, you must plan to modify your product or operations, find a substitute acceptable to your product markets, or raise your prices to your customers.

Suppose you must raise your prices. The prospects for sales to the electronics industry are fine, but will the electronics companies pay more for your products? Will they look for other suppliers or substitute component parts? Knowing in advance what is going to happen next year gives you time to sound out your markets and make modifications; it may mean the difference between keeping and losing your product markets.

Indicators may be brief, but they will tell you a great deal.

If you wanted to open a business in a city of 300,000 people, you would need to know the quantity of your product purchased in that town each year, how much is spent for it (sales volume), how many competitors there are operating in the same town, the market levels in which they sell, and how much of the consumer income is spent on your kind of products or services. *Indicators can tell you.* There are data available to cover all such situations.

Management can tell the future in many ways by reading market indicators. You don't need a crystal ball. You need the facts.

If the economic trends for that town indicated that unemployment was rising steadily, with family incomes dropping over a five-year period, you may reconsider your decision to open a business there. *Indicators can tell you the situation now and in the immediate future.* Any business that fails to keep in touch with the indicators relating to its operation is looking for trouble.

Generally, the sources for indicators are highly accessible and easily followed on a regular basis. These research sources will be discussed in more detail in the next section. Here we will mention only a few of them and show how they can serve your business needs.

Let us first consider the factor markets, in which you buy your supplies and other operational needs.

By monitoring the prices of raw materials used in your products, you can get a clue to changes in prices and supply. *The Wall Street Journal* and the *Survey of Current Business* are two of the many sources for these kinds of data, or indicators.

You can find in these or other sources such indicators as daily listings (quotations) of cash prices of raw materials such as foods, grains, and feeds, fats and oils, textiles and fibers, metals, and miscellaneous products (rubber, hides, gasoline and fuel oil, precious metals, and so on). You can also find listings of future prices of such raw materials, as well as prices and production data for several categories of products. Some sources issue daily reports, others publish on a monthly basis.

Trade and industry journals and trade publications also note prices and production data—plus sales and sales projections for future periods—for various materials and products or services.

Armed with such information, business managers can estimate increased or decreased costs for supplies, identify factor inputs that may be in short supply, and get an idea of current and projected sales and prices of various product lines. They can then plan ahead and modify the business operations as needed to meet current or future changes and trends.

Indicators can also help you estimate changes going on in your product markets. They inform management about forces or influences that can affect the buyers in your factor markets and change their supply or costs.

Indicators extracted from industry news and general trade news may note impending labor problems in certain business or industrial areas, including strikes, labor shortages, labor laws and regulations, labor costs, and other labor-related data which reflect on supply, costs, or working conditions. If labor costs go up in your factor markets, the prices you pay for supplies could well go up, too.

If the costs for fuel or power increase, suppliers in your factor markets which are large energy users may be forced to raise their prices to cover their increased costs. Those increases may be passed along to you. Similarly, regulations and laws governing pollution, safety, or processing and handling may be changed or enforced more strictly than before, causing your suppliers to invest in new equipment or more costly processing procedures. Again, those costs are likely to be passed on to your business.

If unemployment sharply increases in one of your business areas, you may lose sales, be forced to purchase less of certain supplies, and lose discounts and other benefits of bulk purchasing.

Indicators keep your business alert for changes or trends that threaten its stability and balance. They are the eyes and ears of management. They keep you in touch with changes inside and outside the business.

The primary responsibilities for research and monitoring of trends in your product markets lie with the sales and marketing functions of the operation.

The sales and marketing units must determine the purchasing potential of product markets. They must research, canvass, and gather information about the actual product markets, their total dollar purchases, and their purchases in specific market areas and levels. They must determine the share of those markets which the business can expect to capture. (More will be said about these functions in the next chapter.)

Indicators tell about all the considerations you must be aware of to modify your operations to meet new market needs and conditions. They may indicate opportunities to introduce new or modified products or services. They may point to new kinds of businesses that may need your products or services. They may help you find new ways to capture greater share of markets.

Indicators also monitor economic conditions and the buying power of the customers served by your customers. Your products and services may pass through many stages in both factor and product markets after you sell them. If purchasing drops off anywhere down the line in the business process, your business will feel the effects.

Where you find the indicators that are relevant to your business depends to a large degree on the kind of information you seek. In general, however, research and source materials can be found for almost any need. The following section deals with some of the more common sources that may prove useful to you.

Research

Research of business data and information, as we have seen, is critical to business success and profitability. In business competition, no business can afford to be the last to know.

Listen to your business. Listen to messages from outside your business.

If your competitors know about changes or trends before you wake up, they will seize that advantage to capture your markets. Often, the first one to come up with new ideas, systems, products or services is the one that will sweep the market. If management seeks to protect its investment and security, it must make every effort to be informed about changes and trends that affect its business.

Information covering all business needs is readily available. To derive any use from it, however, you must know two things: (1) what information you require, and (2) where to find it.

All business needs for information cannot be found in one place. While much of it can be found in one good library, it will typically be distributed in several books, papers, magazines, and reports. Once management knows where to look for the information it needs, it can quickly find it. Also, knowing what type of data are likely to reveal the most significant information makes the task of research easier and helps management ascertain the business facts it needs to keep in touch with changes and trends. Very often good business information is also found by talking to businesspeople in the same or related industries, or to sales personnel, suppliers, or accountants.

Because business information and data are researched and developed by many different parties for many purposes, it is important to know which party in government, industry, or other sources covers what areas, and where each type of data can be found. Also, it is important to know what business-related information each area offers you and how you can use it.

Management must keep in touch with its factor markets, where it buys its needs.

Information or data that can tell a business about the supply of its needs, now and in the future, is valuable. A business has to know about shortages or surpluses in supply, about prices and quality, about new products and services, about new technology, about new materials, about labor supply, fuel supply, availability of financing, shipping costs, and laws and regulations affecting its supply of goods or services.

There are data and information sources that are researched and developed by government agencies, industry and trade associations, departments of newspapers. On a daily, monthly, or annual basis, these sources provide constant data about factor inputs, whether materials, equipment, or people.

Manpower-related agencies like the Bureau of Labor Statistics publish analyses of the labor force (people working or looking for work), broken down by industries and businesses within industries or

Management must keep in touch with business indicators.

by trades and professions. These sources also note standard wages, projected wage scales, and labor shortages and surpluses, and they even break down such information according to geographical areas. Management can get a good picture of its labor supply and of wage scales, both now and in the future, by reading those reports. They are presented in simple form, allowing easy detection of the relevant indicators.

Government agencies, newspapers, and trade publications also regularly publish data and information about the supply and prices of raw materials and many product and service lines; about expected production rates; about new technology, machines, systems, materials or products that can reduce labor needs, increase production, and reduce costs. Information about supplies and costs of fuel and energy can be obtained from other publications and from fuel and energy suppliers. Certainly, management needs to keep track of its fuel and energy costs if it is to operate profitably.

Similarly, there are numerous government and trade publications, as well as newspapers and news magazines, in which you can find information about current or pending laws and regulations affecting your factor markets. You must be warned in advance about cost increases faced by your suppliers because of changes in the law. Data about real estate and the rental market are also easily available, as is information about trends in transportation and shipping costs that might affect you or your suppliers.

In one place or another, and in many cases in a single source, much of this information can be found. It has already been broken down into simple categories for your use. All you have to do is to go to the source and collect your information, study it, and piece it together with other data that tell you other things about your business prospects and markets.

Management can keep in touch with its product markets, where it sells its products and services.

Before it can plan operations, it must know the size of the *actual product markets* for its products and services and the specific *market area* and *market level* into which its goods and services fall.

It must know if similar products or services are being sold by others, and to what extent customers accept their products and services. It must know the purchasing power and demand in its own product markets and in those of its customers. If your customers cannot sell their own products and services, they cannot buy yours.

It must know what is happening in different business areas it operates in or sells to. If economic conditions are bad in an area, it can affect the sales of your customers or your business. If the area does not have enough demand or buying power, it may be unprofit-

Get the facts. Research is a prime function of management.

able to operate in or sell to that area. If there is strong competition in that area, it may take too much effort to capture a sizable enough piece of the market to make it profitable.

Management must also know what changes are taking place in lifestyles, preferences, needs, and business patterns. If your product market in an area consists of small businesses and they are closing while big businesses are growing, you must either try to sell to big businesses or plan to reduce operations or sales in that area. If customers of yours, or of your customers, decide that they prefer another kind of product or service to yours, or to your customers', it will affect your sales. If laws and regulations affect the sale of your products or services in a particular business area, sales may drop or customer resistance may build.

A business must know all it can about its product markets so it can plan and relate its production, purchases, and needs to estimates of actual product markets and projected sales volumes. All that information can be found, and in brief form, with little trouble.

Management must also know about the general economy, its condition now and in the future. It must know how its factor markets, product markets, and industry will be affected by these broader trends.

A business must know its prospects. Should it expand? Should it pull its belt in? Should it look for new products and services and new markets? What will its needs be next week, next month, and next year?

Indicators can give you clues. They are readily available and easy to find.

Because of the many kinds and sources of data of interest to business, they are broken down into categories to make it easier to locate relevant information. Accordingly, there are geographic indicators, economic indicators, demographic and consumer indicators, manpower indicators, and financial indicators, to name the most common categories.

Geographic indicators, like maps, give the location of cities, towns, and villages, and the distances between them. They specify state, county, and regional boundaries. They tell you about highways, bridges, tunnels, roads, railroads, canals, rivers and lakes, and thereby help you identify access, and means of access, to different places, as well as the mileage of access routes. If a business ships by truck, train, or boat, it can get an idea of mileages and time and cost factors by consulting geographic indicators. Similarly, if air transport is to be used, geographic indicators tell about airports and mileages.

There are geographic indicators available for almost any area, no matter what its size. A business may sell to a city, a state, a group of

STATES

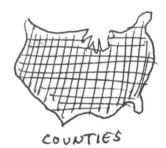

COUNTIES

STANDARD METROPOLITAN AREAS

REGIONS

states, a county, or a region made up of parts of cities, counties, and states. In order to get information about its areas of operation, whether they are small or large, the business must first define the geographical boundaries of those areas; once this is done, it is an easy matter to locate the appropriate indicators.

Major geographic areas in the United States include national areas (the whole country), state areas (whole states), county areas, Standard Metropolitan Statistical Areas (which include a population center, like a major city, and the immediately surrounding area that is part of its economic zone), cities, towns, villages, and townships.

There are regions made up of several states, which are well-established economic areas in the nation. For instance, the New England Region includes Connecticut, Maine, Massachusetts, New Hampshire, Rhode Island, and Vermont. The Mid-Atlantic Region includes New Jersey, New York, and Pennsylvania. The West-South Central Region includes Alabama, Kentucky, Mississippi, and Tennessee.

The New York Standard Metropolitan Statistical Area (SMSA) is centered in New York City and covers part of New Jersey, Connecticut, Long Island, and Westchester County; all are part of an interrelated economic area. There are many businesses operating in this area, and the labor force serving those businesses is spread out over various parts of the area.

Maps of the United States and of different areas within the United States can be found in most libraries. Once you have identified the particular area with which you are concerned and the region, state, county, municipality, or other that most closely matches its boundaries, other data you need can be found by referring to information noted in research sources that refer to the same area by name. For instance, if the area you are concerned with is best matched to the Mid-Atlantic Region, then look for data about economics, labor, markets, and so on under Mid-Atlantic Region in other sources, or under the names of the states in the Mid-Atlantic Region—New York, New Jersey, and Pennsylvania.

Another important category of indicators are **economic indicators.** They tell you details about the economic activity in the nation, regions, states, and cities of the United States or other countries. Economic indicators give you information about broad industrial groups, such as agriculture, forestry, fishing, mining, construction, or manufacturing, and the many groups within them, for instance, the lumber, steel, or automobile industries. They also tell you about businesses within particular industries by types, such as manufacturing, supply, wholesale, distribution, retail, or service, and about different kinds of businesses within each type.

From these indicators, you can learn how many businesses there are in broad industrial areas, in particular industrial groups, and in

Check your indicators. Set real measures for your plans.

the different types. They tell you how much business each category did in the past and is expected to do in the future, in both dollar amounts and quantity. They inform you where the concentrations of customers of all kinds and levels are located, how many people they employ, how much they purchase in factor markets, and what their operating costs are.

Economic indicators tell you, in terms of quantity or dollars, about the purchases by customers in various categories, including the machinery and equipment they buy. They compare purchases in the past with current purchases and expected purchases.

As we said earlier, economic indicators tell you about both factor and product markets. They detail the supply or production of raw materials and intermediate or finished goods, their costs in the past and the future. They warn you in advance of shortages or surpluses in supply and tell you about sales of particular products or services, by area and amounts. They identify the organizations that buy particular products and services, and the amounts they buy.

Demographic and **consumer indicators** tell you about the social and economic patterns in population centers and various areas. They describe the populations in these areas by age and sex and specify the number of individuals, families, and households. Also, they give information about incomes, taxes and other deductions from incomes, disposable incomes (money from income after deductions), and the amounts and kinds of products and services purchased with disposable incomes. All of this information is broken down by geographical area, industry, business, business type, and other useful categories.

Demographic and consumer indicators provide a picture of the population makeup, the countries of origin of people in the area, their education, skills, occupations, wages, union membership, the number employed or unemployed by age, sex and country of origin (ethnic group). They tell you where the people work, shop, and travel, and what their lifestyles, social patterns, interests, preferences, and needs are.

Demographic and consumer indicators can tell you all that information about the nation, a state, a region, a county, or just one city block.

Demographic and consumer indicators are important because they inform you about the buying power and demand for goods and services in particular areas, the labor supply, the number of people, the way they spend their money, and how much is spent on different products and services. They may be your customers or those of your customers. Who they are, what they buy, how much they spend, what they prefer—all this can affect your business.

Manpower indicators tell you about the labor supply, the number of people in the labor force (employed or looking for work) in different areas, their skills, the number of people with specific skills in different business areas, the number in demand in various areas, and labor shortages or surpluses. They tell you about current and projected wage scales and the kinds of businesses you may be competing with for the same labor supply. They give you an idea of the ethnic makeup of the labor force, its ages, sex, and education, and of changes in these factors. They tell you how far and by what means they travel to work and how much time and money they pay for commuting. You can learn how many people work in different industries and businesses and in what occupational levels they work.

Finally, **financial indicators** inform you about such things as interest rates for financing, the money supply, or the amount of loans made by lending institutions. There are many other kinds of indicators dealing with specific businesses or aspects of operations and trade. The ones described here are those that are most important to the majority of small businesses.

Indicators are presented in many forms. They may use statistics (numbers and percentages), verbal descriptions, and comparisons.

Statistical indicators, which make use of mathematical methods, note numerical amounts—say, 5,000,000 units or 10,000 tons or 62,000 barrels. They also use percentages, such as 60 percent of sales, 50 percent of production, or 20 percent of gross sales. *Descriptive indicators* tell you in words such things as "Sales increased over the last month," "The market for electronic equipment has softened," or "It is feared that a strike could have disastrous effects on the industry." Combined statistical and descriptive indicators might say something like "The industry sold 6,000,000 units last year, but because of a strike in the early part of this year, sales will not exceed 5,000,000 units."

Certain special terms are frequently used in statistical presentations, and it is important to understand them if any benefit is to come from statistical indicators. One such term is "per capita," which simply means "per person." If a statistical table said that the amount of sugar used each year was 50 pounds per capita, it would mean that on an average (some more and some less), each person uses 50 pounds of sugar a year. If the per capita income of a town of 1,000 persons is $1,000 a year, the total income for all persons is $1,000 times 1,000 persons, or $1,000,000. If you knew that the total income for the town was $1,000,000 and that it had 1,000 people, you could figure out the per capita income by dividing $1,000,000 by 1,000, which gives you $1,000 per person.

Another term commonly used is "median." Median refers to that point where one half of an amount being measured lies above (is more than) the point, and one half lies below (is less than). For instance, if seven persons worked for a business and one worker were paid $1,000, one $2,000, one $3,000, one $4,000, one $5,000, one $6,000, and one $7,000, the "median" wage would be $4,000 since half fall above that point and half fall below it. The concept applies in the same way to sales, tons purchased, number of persons employed in different levels of a business, and a host of other measures.

"Seasonally adjusted" is another phrase you will see in many charts. This means that the data have been adjusted to allow for seasonal variations. Certain businesses, like the soda companies, do more business in the summer months; others, like the coal business, do better in the winter. In presenting data about those businesses, the data are adjusted to account for the differences in sales in the months when certain products or services are in season.

"Index" is yet another word you will find often used. An index measures changes that have taken place over a period of time in different things, such as prices or sales. One period of time, generally a year, is picked as a standard, and other years are measured against it. For instance, let us say that auto sales in 1968 were 10,000,000 cars. This may be used as our base year. If car sales in 1969 were 12,000,000 cars, then 2,000,000 more cars were sold in 1969 than in 1968. Converted into percentages, 20 percent more cars were sold in 1969 than in 1968, and it could be said that sales in 1969, using 1968 as an index, were 120 percent of cars sold in 1968. The base year, as the example makes clear, is counted as 100 percent; add 20 percent for the increase in 1969, and the 1969 index is 120 percent. If in 1970, sales rose to 14,000,000 cars, they would be 40 percent higher than sales in 1968, and the index for 1970 would be 140 percent.

The index of sales for your business might look as follows:

Year	Sales	%
1970	$ 50,000	100 (base year)
1971	$ 60,000	120
1972	$ 80,000	160
1973	$100,000	200
1974	$ 80,000	160

Sources for such specific kinds of data and information can be most easily located if you look for it by category—geographic, economic, demographic, manpower, or financial. Certain research materials (books, magazines, reports, and so on) specialize in one or the other of these categories. The following examples will illustrate the research sources and techniques that can be used by management.

Economic indicator sources. For the purpose of establishing standard codes for different industries, kinds of businesses, and levels of businesses, the United States has adopted several coding systems, of which the Standard Industrial Classification, SIC Code for short, is among the most widely accepted. Using a number system, broad industrial groups are broken into specific industrial groups and then into kinds and levels of business activity within groups.

For instance, Commercial Printing, Letterpress, and Screen Establishments would be SIC Code #2751. The first two numbers, *27*, refer to the major industrial group (manufacturing); *5* refers to the group within the major group (commercial printing); and the last digit, *1*, represents the specific group within that group (commercial printing, letterpress, and screen establishments). Another example of the way the SIC system works would be Commercial Printing (SIC #275) and related businesses, such as Commercial Printing, Lithographic, (SIC #2752), and Engraving and Plate Printing (SIC #2753).

Data are also classified in terms of durable and nondurable products. Durable generally refers to the ''hard goods'' such as machinery or equipment, and nondurable to the ''soft goods'' such as food or clothing.

You can find your SIC Code number by referring to the Standard Industrial Classification Book at your library.

For information and data about factor and product markets, prices, production, sales, and forecasts, broken down by area, industry, and kind of business, the following sources (which are only a very small sample of the many that are available) are noted for your reference.

Survey of Current Business. Published monthly by the United States Department of Commerce, Bureau of Economic Analysis.

U.S. Industrial Outlook Published annually by the United States Department of Commerce, Bureau of Domestic and International Business Administration.

1972 Census of: Wholesale Trade; Selected Services Industries; Construction Industries; Retail Trade; Manufacturing; Mineral Industries; Transportation. Published by the United States Department of Commerce, Social and Economic Statistics Administration, Bureau of the Census. Each census is comprised of many volumes in each category, providing information by state and industry groups.

Thomas Register of American Manufacturers and *Thomas Register Catalog File*. Published annually by the Thomas Publishing Company, New York.

Predicasts. Published by Predicasts, Inc., 11001 Cedar Avenue, Cleveland, Ohio 44106.

The Wall Street Journal.

State Industrial Directories. Published by the State Industrial Directory Corporation, 2 Penn Plaza, New York, N.Y. 10001.

Dun & Bradstreet Middle Market Directory. Published by Dun & Bradstreet, Inc., 99 Church Street, New York, N.Y. 10007.

Area Economic Projections 1990. Published by the United States Department of Commerce, Social and Economic Statistics Administration, Bureau of Economic Analysis.

Dun & Bradstreet Million Dollar Directory. Published by Dun & Bradstreet, Inc.

Standard & Poor's Register of Corporations, Directors, and Executives. Published by Standard & Poors Corp., 345 Hudson Street, New York, N.Y. 10014.

Economic Indicators can also be found in publications of your local Department of Commerce, local Chamber of Commerce, and local business or trade associations.

Demographic indicator sources. There are many sources of information about demographic characteristics of areas. Most local or state governments publish studies based on census figures, as does the federal government. The following are some sources for such data.

General Population Characteristics (Series). Published for each state separately by the United States Department of Commerce, Bureau of Census.

General Social and Economic Characteristics (Series). Published for each state separately by the United States Department of Commerce, Social and Economic Statistics Administration and Bureau of Census.

U.S. Department of Commerce, Bureau of Census, 1970 Census Data. Publications of local, state, and community data for any area in the U.S.

Various local, state, and community publications put out by agencies such as health, police, fire, welfare, community development, and labor departments.

Manpower indicators can be found in publications of the Bureau of Labor Statistics, United States Department of Labor. They cover all business areas with which you may be concerned. Also, publications of local, state, and community agencies deal with labor statistics and related data.

Specific business indicators can also be found in publications of business and trade associations, and in the materials distributed by manufacturers and suppliers.

The process of research may be strange to you at the beginning, but do not get discouraged. Your efforts will pay off.

Like looking for an unfamiliar address, looking for information in libraries and other sources can be strange to you. Once you locate it, however, the rest is easy. If you have difficulties locating research materials, ask your librarian for assistance or call the commerce department offices of the different branches of government. All parties will give you their cooperation. The same holds true for community agencies, trade associations, and others.

The following examples may illustrate the significance of indicators.

Example #1

Suppose that you are a manufacturer of component parts used in the electronics industry, the home-appliance industry, the leisure industry, and the office-equipment industry.

Within the electronics industry, your products are used in the radio market areas, and they are in a high market level (expensive sets). Within the home-appliance industry, they are used in the washing-machine area in a medium level. They are sold to the boat market area of the leisure industry, in the lower level (small craft). Finally, they are used in the calculator market area of the office-equipment industry, in a medium level (desk-top models).

In analyzing your sales, which total $2 million a year, you find that sales to the electronics industry were $1 million, sales to the home-appliance industry were $200,000, sales to the office-equipment industry were $500,000, and sales to the leisure industry were $300,000.

Your product is made of copper and plastics. You note that the price of copper has been rising over the past few years and continues to rise this year. Projections indicate that it will rise next year at the same rate. It cost $0.64 a pound in 1975, $0.73 a pound in 1976, and indicators forecast a cost of $0.85 a pound in 1977. That means that the cost of your materials will rise, and unless you can modify your product or your operations, you will be forced to raise the prices of your products. Plastics remain constant.

You also note that wages for the kind of labor you employ, on the same skill levels, or in the same unions, have been rising. To get the quality labor you need, you must pay higher wages. Forecasts show that there will be a strong demand for such labor in the next few years, and wages will rise with demand. You must figure these higher labor costs into your planning.

Research tells you that the cost of fuel has been rising at a rate of 10 percent a year and will continue to rise for the next several years. You therefore must allow for higher fuel costs in your planning.

By examining all of the factor inputs of your business, one at a time, you arrive at the conclusion that your overall costs, including all factor inputs, will rise at a rate of 10 percent a year for next year and the year thereafter. That means that you must either reduce other costs or raise prices. If you sold your products for the same prices and did not reduce costs, you would have to absorb the 10 percent increase and may not show profits after costs.

Now you study your product markets.

You note that the electronics industry has overproduced and that demand has dropped for home appliances and home electronic products because of the drop in homebuilding. Forecasts indicate that next year's sales of home appliances and home electronic products—in your case, washing machines and radios—will be 20 percent lower than this year.

However, projections for the leisure industry indicate that boat sales will rise by 10 percent next year. The sales levels for the office-equipment industry are expected to remain stable.

You are now faced with a problem. Sales of your product for use in washing machines or radios may drop next year. This does not mean that they will necessarily drop, but if you feel the effects of lower general industry sales, your sales will drop to some degree. Sales to the boat builders could increase, whereas sales to the calculator manufacturers may be expected to remain constant.

With demand projected to drop in two of your four product-market areas, and your rising costs placing your business in a position where it may have to increase prices, your two weak market areas may react strongly to increased prices, reducing sales even further. What can you do?

Since sales of boats will rise and those of calculators will remain stable, those markets will be better able to pay increased prices and sustain demand. You could identify other manufacturers of these products to broaden your sales to those market areas.

You could also review your product design, your operating costs, your sources of supply, your labor needs, and so on to see where you could cut costs to keep the price stable or avoid a drastic increase. The lower the price, the better the acceptance in your depressed market areas.

The important thing is that you are aware of the problems and have hard facts to work with. Without these facts, you cannot modify your plans and operations effectively and will fail in the long run. Research provides you with the tools you need to adapt to the market situation.

Example #2
You are a wholesaler of houseware products and want to expand your business area to include the state of New Jersey. You now operate in New York State only.

PRODUCT MARKETS
WHOLE PIE

MARKET AREA
HALF THE PIE

MARKET LEVEL
SMALL PIECE OF PIE

YOUR SHARE OF
TOTAL MARKETS

To implement your plan, you want to establish a warehouse in New Jersey from which to service that new market area. *How do you go about identifying your actual markets in New Jersey, and where do you locate your warehouse?*

First, you study the economic, geographic, and demographic indicators and your potential competition. (The figures used in this example are not actual but are used for illustrative purposes only.)

You find that there are 11 million people residing in New Jersey, in 3 million households, with total incomes of $35 billion and disposable incomes of $25 billion. You find that total houseware sales in New Jersey last year totalled $3 billion and that there are 150 houseware suppliers (wholesalers) listed in the state of New Jersey. You also learn that wholesale sales of housewares totalled $2 billion last year.

Because of the increase in homebuilding, you note from indicators, the number of households will increase by 150,000 next year and the demand for houseware items will increase by 5 percent over last year. You learn that most middle-income and upper-income homes are concentrated in certain areas. Furthermore, you find that there are 1,000 retailers of housewares, not counting major department stores. Major department stores in New Jersey, however, account for 30 percent of all houseware sales, or 30 percent of the total sales of $3 billion, with the remainder distributed among the 1,000 independent retailers. That tells you that department stores sell $900 million worth of housewares, and independents sell the rest.

You study the road and highway systems to find a central location near major facilities. What you are interested in are commercial highways, rail systems, a good labor supply, and a stable business area. You learn that certain areas have been deteriorating while others are stable or being renewed and redeveloped. Some new industrial sites are available in stable business areas.

Then you study retail figures. You learn that houseware retailers' sales in your particular product area (say, bathroom items) amount to 10 percent of all sales. That means that overall, your kind of products accounts for 10 percent of the total $3 billion in retail sales (or for $300 million), and for roughly 10 percent (about $200 million) of wholesale purchases. You know major department stores account for 30 percent of all sales and roughly 30 percent of all purchases, and therefore that the independent market for your products amounts to 10 percent of 70 percent of wholesale sales, or 10 percent of $140 million, namely $14 million a year.

There are 150 competitors in the state selling to that same market, but from your research you learn that of those wholesalers, only 100 sell the same or similar products as yours. Thus, if the *market area* to which you sell accounts for $14 million a year in purchases and that amount were distributed evenly over the 100 suppliers, each would sell approximately $140,000 worth of housewares to the bathroom-items market area. However, there are different *market levels* in that market area.

You sell a higher-priced line, and that accounts for only 40 percent of the wholesale purchases in your market area. If only 50 of the 100 wholesalers which are your competitors sell to that same level, you all share 40 percent of the purchases of bathroom items by independent retailers, or $5.6 million a year. Distributed over 50 suppliers evenly, each would sell $112,000 a year on an average.

When you compute the costs of renting a warehouse, purchasing or renting trucks, hiring labor, and all other factor inputs and operating costs, you find that you need a certain sales volume to recover costs and earn profits. Let us say that for you to operate successfully, you determine that you must have sales in New Jersey of about $1 million a year. That means that you must capture approximately 18 percent of the sales of $5.6 million in your market area and market level.

You must determine through marketing procedures (discussed in the next chapter) whether the demand for your products by the houseware retailers in New Jersey is strong enough to enable you to sell $1 million worth of your products.

While data do not always tell you the whole story or in any way guarantee success, they give you the information that can help you determine the best course for your business, help you keep it balanced and profitable and maximize opportunities as they develop.

Without researching indicators, management cannot make sound business judgments or investments.

4

Marketing, Production, and Sales

The marketing, production, and sales functions are very closely related because they all deal directly with products and services: the marketing function identifies the specific markets, needs, and preferences; the production function generates the products or services to satisfy those specific needs and preferences; and the sales function deals directly with the business's customers to obtain the sales levels needed to achieve profitability.

The interrelationships and the contributions of the three functions to one another will be defined in the following. The first step must be the identification of markets—of the customers that are ready and able to buy specific goods and services within established business areas.

Marketing

Marketing is the function of a business that seeks to get the right product or service to the right customer, at the right place and time and for the right price and sales terms.

Translated into the language learned in previous chapters, that means that the function (and person assigned to that function) of marketing is to identify customers in product markets that have a strong demand for your kinds of products and services, are interested in buying those

Marketing means getting the right product or service to the right customer at the right place and time and for the right price and sales terms.

products and services, are willing and able to pay for them, can meet your sales terms and conditions, and will accept your prices as competitive. Also, your products and services must fall into clearly defined market areas and levels within those product markets and be delivered when customers want them, and be in sufficient supply to meet their business needs.

There is flexibility in marketing. Your products and services may meet strong demand as they are, or they may require some modifications. They may meet demand in new product markets, market areas, and market levels in unchanged or modified form. Entirely new products or services may have to be developed and offered to meet identified demand in old or new markets, areas, or levels.

In all instances, the function of marketing remains basically the same: to get the right products and services to the right customer, at the right time and place and for the right price and sales terms.

Every business needs a marketing function, which must be filled by a staff member and tied to management systems and controls and to systems of communication and reporting.

Whether a business has three employees or three hundred, marketing is critical to business success. A qualified person must be assigned to manage that function and be responsible for reporting, record maintenance, control of systems, and development and research. That person may or may not be performing other functions as well. In a small business, one person may be both the marketing and the sales manager. In a larger business, one person may concentrate on the marketing function alone and have a staff working under him or her.

The person performing the marketing function is part of the management team.

Whoever is reponsible for marketing must sit with management to participate in planning, budgeting, and modifying operations to meet changes and needs. The marketing manager must supply market data and information, examine and review market indicators, and conduct market research.

In big business, products and services produced and sold are not selected or offered by chance. Big business tries not to gamble. Small business is no different in this; it cannot afford to gamble.

It is not enough to like your own products or services; you're not the one who is buying them. The *customer* must like them, need them, and be willing to pay a certain price for them. The marketing function researches the needs and demands of customers in your product markets, taking into consideration the kinds of products or services the business currently offers for sale, as well as those it may add to its lines. This research will often have to cover many kinds of businesses in many different industrial groups, and it typically must consider the needs of individuals as well as organizations. Frequently, the needs and demands identified by marketing will point to the necessity of introducing new or modified products so as to remain competitive.

It is easier to match products and services to actual needs and demands in actual product markets than to match actual markets to already defined products and services.

In brief, it is easier to design or modify products and services to meet your product markets' needs than it is to find buyers who are ready to accept your products or services as you present them. Before investing money, time, labor, and materials, know whether there is enough market demand for certain products and services. If there are too few customers for your goods or services, you cannot stay in business long.

Your first task in marketing is to identify the right buyers and the products and services they demand. When that is accomplished, you can concern yourself with such other issues as pricing, sales, terms, delivery demands, or quality control.

The fact that you have products and services does not mean that a strong product market exists for them. Similarly, because a strong market demand exists for your kinds of products and services, it does not follow that you can meet the demand, or the conditions of sale, to capture a piece of that market.

Marketing matches the needs of both the business and its product markets. It identifies the buyers, measures their potentials as customers, evaluates their demand and buying power, matches products and services to specific needs, and seeks profitable ways to match competition and capture new customers.

Marketing is matchmaking. It evaluates potentials for sales and seeks to convert these potentials into actual sales.

Working through research and the study of indicators, it identifies industries, industrial groups, businesses, individuals, and others that use the type of products or services you sell. Based on that study, it determines the best matches between your and your customers' needs.

This does not happen by itself. Marketing requires research, analysis, and planning; it means looking at a product or service as

What is the demand for your products or services?

both a producer and a user—that is, from the point of view of both the business and the customer. It means planning and implementing changes where they are necessary to meet the demand of identified and interested product markets.

Marketing means that a business must find out all it can about its customers and their customers, both actual and potential, and make plans to best meet their needs, wants, and conditions as to products or services. Marketing must identify and analyze the business areas in which the customers are located, and it must estimate the costs of delivering products and services to those areas. It must find out when and in what amounts particular products are needed and develop plans for meeting those delivery demands. And it is responsible for identifying methods to reduce prices in order to open new product markets and fill new demands or needs.

As we have mentioned, marketing must view products and services from two different points of view: that of the business and that of the customer. Without this, the business cannot match the needs of its product markets and operate profitably.

The business views its products and services in terms of production, labor, facilities, management, machinery and equipment, supplies, and overall costs, as well as its sales prices and gross revenues.

The customer evaluates products and services in terms of usefulness, quality, price, style, and so on. If the customer is a business, it is concerned with sales terms, delivery, quantities, regulations, compatibility with laws and regulations, prices, and product specifications, because all these will affect its own costs, production, and ability to sell to its own product markets at a competitive price. If your customers are consumers, they will more likely be concerned only with styles, comparative prices, quality, delivery terms, and the urgency of their need.

To make a good match, sellers and buyers must be satisfied. Both must benefit, and both must get what they need and when they need it.

Consider the right and wrong way to do business.

Company A manufactures bicycles. Without conducting a marketing study, it designed a line of bicycles to be retailed for $150 to $200 a piece and immediately began production of its products.

Its salespersons contacted businesses that sell bicycles and attempted to sell the products. In some cases they were successful, but because of the high retail price for the quality bicycles, sales were

Don't just try to sell products and services. Make sure that there is demand for them and that your markets have the buying power to purchase them, or you will get stuck with huge inventories.

small to each customer. Other customers examined the bicycles and concluded that they were overpriced for their customers. Also, many noted that the heights offered were not varied enough to meet their full market demand, for both children's and adults' bicycles. In short, sales generated were not enough to carry the business, and its future was threatened.

Company B, on the other hand, studied the markets for bicycles. The marketing department talked to the bicycle retailers to determine those styles and price levels most in demand by their customers. It examined the products of competitors to determine the kind of value, styling, materials, sizes, and so on offered by others. It analyzed the seasonal demands of retailers and the terms and conditions of sale offered by other manufacturers and suppliers. It studied the kinds of businesses, aside from bicycle stores, that sold bicycles and visited those establishments to get facts. It made a thorough study of the *indicators* for the leisure industry and determined how many and what kinds of bicycles were sold last year, and at what prices. It studied the potentials for sales in the next few years. It read trade and sports magazines and trade journals to determine changing consumer preferences, color choices, and the benefits of one structural material over another.

When it had gathered all of its information and data and selected the appropriate indicators, it concluded that the business should concentrate on bicycles of certain styles and sizes, made of particular materials, with certain styling and colors. They were to retail for prices of $50 to $75 for junior sizes and $90 to $125 for adult sizes. Decals and flags were included to meet strong consumer interest in bicycle racing.

When Company B went out to sell its bicycles, it sold a storm. The product markets, both in bicycle stores and other retail operations, responded with enthusiasm. The styling and sizing were right. The price was right. The materials were right. The image was timely.

Marketing paid off. It gave customers what they needed and wanted for the right price.

In its research, Company B discovered that consumers buy bicycles for a variety of purposes, for instance, for transport, for exercise, or for racing in competition. Also, the consumer markets ranged from children to persons advanced in age.

Taking advantage of this knowledge, Company B developed a line of bicycles directed at these different consumer market areas. It came out with special bikes for speed racing, for older folks, and for exercise (on stands). The expanded markets opened up new business without affecting the original products or services. The company found opportunities through marketing, and it seized them.

How does your business operate—like Company A or Company B?

Marketing must be in continuous direct contacts with the customers of the business. Never assume that you know the answers. Never think for your actual or potential product markets. Let them tell you. Put that information together with research of indicators, and you have a good picture of your business prospects.

Big companies give out free samples for testing. They interview consumers on street corners or call them at their homes. They ask questions about needs, wants, price, preferences, age, sex, and education. They want to know the characteristics of customers in order to determine which ones prefer certain kinds of products, and the prices they are willing to pay for them. They contact businesses in their product markets and ask them a range of questions so as to identify the kinds of products or services in a product or service line that are most in demand in particular market areas and levels.

You too must get the facts before you move. Although you cannot be right in every case, you can cut your risks down. Follow the procedures laid out for you in the sections on *indicators* and *research*. Your efforts will prove to be well invested.

If you are already in business and selling products and services, this is the time to start marketing. If your competitors have marketing departments that do their job, and you do not, your prospects for holding your product markets are poor, and your prospects for expansion are even worse.

Diversifying your product lines and markets is a safeguard. It helps overcome changes in any one product market.

In our previous example about bicycle manufacturers, Company A had one line of products directed at a single market area and level in one kind of product market. Company B, by contrast, had several lines of products directed at different market areas on different levels. If the customers of Company A stopped buying its products, the company would die because it only sold a limited line to one market.

On the other hand, if the customers of Company B stopped buying racing bikes, others might still be buying bikes for health or exercises purposes or as means of transport. If adults stopped buying, children might continue to buy. If bicycle retailers suffered drops in sales, department stores and hardware stores might still be selling. Company B, in other words, is not dependent on one product, one market area or level, or one kind of customer.

Businesses must identify, categorize, and weigh their diversified markets.

Don't gamble with your business. Get the facts and play it smart.

Let us say you sell bicycles for children and adults. Your different models are used for recreation, exercise, racing, and transport (these, then, are your market areas), and their prices range from $50 to $150. You sell your products to bicycle stores and department stores. Your business areas are New York, New Jersey, and Pennsylvania.

Your marketing department must determine the sales potentials of your different products in each market area, market level, and business area. Besides studying its own product markets, it must also determine the composition of the final markets (customers of your customers).

First it will determine the size and potentials of the product markets in the different business areas, in the ways described in the section on research in Chapter 3. From that study it can determine your potential market share in the different business areas. It must also determine your potential share in the different market areas and levels. The result of this research may look as in Table 1. According to those figures, the business has the potential to capture, for example, 10 percent of the sales of low-price recreational bicycles in department stores in New York, or 9 percent of the sales of high-price racing bicycles in bicycle stores in Pennsylvania.

You now have a strategic map of your business areas. It tells you about the amount of sales you may expect in different business areas and market areas and levels, considering the number of other suppliers, their prices and sales terms, and the market demand and buying power in each area. By translating these percentages into

Table 1. The business's potential percent shares of actual markets.

Market Areas	New York Business Area		New Jersey Business Area		Pennsylvania Business Area	
	Market Levels (Price Ranges)		Market Levels (Price Ranges)		Market Levels	
	Low	High	Low	High	Low	High
Recreation						
Department Stores	10%		15%		10%	
Bicycle Stores	5%	10%	10%	5%	15%	10%
Exercise						
Department Stores	20%	10%	25%	15%	20%	10%
Bicycle Stores	10%	15%	15%	5%	15%	5%
Racing						
Department Stores	15%	10%	10%	10%	15%	20%
Bicycle Stores	20%	15%	20%	15%	15%	9%
Transport						
Department Stores	10%	5%	10%	—	20%	10%
Bicycle Stores	15%	5%	10%	5%	15%	5%

dollar values, you can estimate the potential demand for each of your products.

Production must conform to the estimated sales patterns. For instance, it would show bad business sense to produce more bicycles of type A than of type B if your marketing study indicated that there are more customers for type-B bicycles. Also, your marketing study helps you determine the kinds and amounts of factor inputs you must purchase in your factor markets to meet customer demand.

Your marketing research may indicate that competition is heavy in a particular business area and light in another, or it may show that for various reasons—say, because of certain characteristics of your product line—your chances of capturing a significant market share are better in one business area than another. This helps you direct your efforts toward your areas of strength so as to build product markets and sales. If an area cannot generate enough to make your operations profitable, it should be cut out, or alternative techniques of selling should be explored—for instance, you may have to switch to using distributors or representatives.

Businesses should always move toward their areas of strength. To make their products or services known to potential users, they must use a variety of methods, such as direct contacts (direct selling), advertising and promotion, or working through sales representatives, distributors, and wholesalers or jobbers. People cannot buy something if they do not know it is available for sale.

The more persons pushing your products or services in different business areas, the better your chance for sales. And the more ways used to make your products or services known to potential customers, the greater your business potentials.

Direct contact by salespersons is an effective method because the salesperson can answer questions, determine needs, and try to make a deal through some formula. A sales force, even if it consists of a single person, is necessary to meet with potential customers, match products and services, and arrange delivery schedules and terms.

Advertising in newspapers and trade magazines, as well as direct mail advertising, is also effective and rewarding. Advertising is a way to get information about your products and services to a lot of people at one time.

Advertising is generally expensive and is effective only if the advertisement appears in the right newspaper or magazine. You must know what kind of readers a newspaper or magazine has so you can determine whether or not they fall in the product markets for your products or services. Certainly a meat market would not want to advertise in an automobile trade magazine. Similarly, a supplier of men's apparel would not ordinarily want to advertise in a woman's magazine.

Don't be a dunce. Without research and planning, no business can operate soundly.

Don't keep your products and services a mystery. Let your customers know what you sell. They cannot buy what they do not know exists.

There are many magazines of all kinds. Some may be good for your advertising, and some bad. Each magazine or newspaper can give you a rundown on its markets (readers) so you can pick the ones best for your business.

For certain types of businesses, radio or television advertising pays off best. The markets are large, and the number of potential customers that see and hear about your products or services number in the thousands or even millions. The costs for this kind of advertising are high. They may be within reach of your business, however, and you should check on this point with your radio and television stations. They, too, have a profile of the people watching or listening at different times so that you can pick the time best suited for your type of customer. Different times cost different amounts.

Advertising may also be done through posters on billboards and through printed flyers, which may be distributed in the street or placed in mail boxes.

The costs of advertising in any form must be measured against the financial resources of the business, and they must be figured in your budgets and recovered as part of overall costs in your sales price.

The specific kind of advertising used will vary with the type of business and its products or services. You may want to push the durability or strength of your products, their attractiveness, their broad or specialized use. No matter what the form of your advertising, it should emphasize the best sales points of your product or service—those features that would make people or businesses want to buy it. To derive any benefit from your advertising, you must identify the unique advantages that set your product off from your competitors. They are the points to be stressed, for they are the ones that will make the customer buy from you rather than from the competition.

Sometimes, wholesalers that purchase your products may agree to advertise them in their promotional material if they feel they can sell a lot and earn good profits. The same holds true for distributors and agents, which will be dealt with in the section on sales in this chapter.

Make some noise in your markets. Let your markets hear about your products and services through advertising and promotion.

Customers also want to know that your products and services are uniform in quality. If people find they cannot rely on your products' having the same quality level each time they buy them, your sales will suffer.

Quality control, discussed in the section on production later in this chapter, ensures uniform standards of quality and workmanship. Much of your business will probably depend on repeat sales, and if your customers begin to question the uniformity of the quality of your products, they will not buy them. If you buy a pen that works well, you are likely to ask for the same brand when you need another one. If the second pen you buy turns out to be of poor quality, you will probably switch to a new brand the third time.

For this reason, it is wise to appoint an employee as "complaint manager" or "customer-service representative." Management must be informed about product complaints so that it can take some corrective action. Certain complaints may point to general weaknesses of your products, and you may have to do something to improve them. Besides that, however, customer satisfaction is important to you. The complaint department enables you to keep your customers happy, be it through refunds or through replacements of damaged products.

A business, as we have said, must sell its products or services in the right place and at the right time.

Most kinds of businesses have products and services that can be sold in many places across the country or even overseas. This does not mean that every business can afford to sell in every place, or that it can find buyers or meet the competition in every place.

A business must define its business areas. They may be a single neighborhood for a small retailer, many neighborhoods for the retailer in a central shopping district, or an entire city for a department store. They may be parts of a city or entire cities, regions, states, counties, or metropolitan areas.

The selection of your business areas depends strictly on two factors. One, they must provide sufficient sales at the right prices and terms for you to recover your costs and earn profits. Two, you must be able to meet the demands of the product markets in these areas, in terms of both quantity and quality.

In some cases, the area that is best for you may be far away from the location of the business. You may be able to sell your goods around the corner, but if you cannot charge prices that cover your costs and allow for a profit, you may be better off selling to an area a thousand miles away. Profitability, not convenience, is your main concern.

Your business must sell not only to the right areas but also to the right markets within those areas. Through sound research, the marketing function must find the business areas with the best sales potentials and identify the prime buyers of your products or services.

If you sold food items, you would not try to sell your products to shoe retailers. Each business must select potential customers that are best for selling particular kinds of products or services. Only in this way can it increase its sales and profits.

For instance, if a bicycle manufacturer researched an area and found that there was high consumer demand for its products and little competition in its product markets and market areas and levels, that area would be a likely choice for a concentrated sales effort. If within that area there were bicycle stores, department stores, and health spas or gymnasiums interested in purchasing its products, there would be a good chance for the business to develop product markets that are prime movers of its products.

In most cases, your prime product markets are high-volume businesses that sell goods or services of your type. A supplier of food products, for instance, could sell more of its products through a supermarket located in a busy marketplace than through ten small grocery stores in small neighborhood shopping areas.

But prime product markets not only buy and sell more, they often enable you to keep costs of shipping and handling low. They buy in large quantities, and because shipments are large, the cost of shipping per item sold is reduced. By contrast, if a customer buys in small quantities and needs frequent shipments, the costs of shipping and handling are high; delivery is more time- and fuel-consuming, and billing and bookkeeping are more costly. Through proper selection of customers, then, you can reduce your operating costs.

You should still diversify your product markets, but in doing so, you must apply the same considerations. Diversification is not a goal in itself; any market or customer you select must enable you to make a profit, and high-volume businesses will generally be preferable to small customers.

In summary, sound management selects business areas not for convenience or because of personal preferences but rather on the basis of demand, sales potentials, levels of competition, buying power, volume sales potentials of product markets, and the demand and buying power of their customers. You cannot force a business area to meet your needs. You must meet the needs of a business area.

Not only must a business select the business areas, product markets, and potential customers that are best for it, it also must determine the time when those markets are most interested in buying its products or services and most willing and able to pay for them.

Some products and services, such as snow shovels, sleds, Christmas lights, fur items, short-sleeved shirts, air conditioners, or garden tools, are seasonal in nature. Others benefit from consumer interest at certain periods of the year. The greeting card business, for instance, makes most of its retail sales in four or five weeks of the year, during such holiday periods as Easter, Christmas, Mother's Day, or Valentine's Day. Similarly, the apparel industry does most of its retail sales in early spring and early fall.

Furniture sales generally rise in the fall season and decline toward the summer. Some sports items generally sell more toward spring and summer and drop during the winter season, whereas others follow the opposite trend.

Manufacturing and distribution peak seasons generally come two to four months before retail seasons in the same product areas. For instance, the apparel manufacturers do most of their selling in the months from February to July, months before retail sales reach their peak. In some industries, purchases are made almost a year before the manufacture or delivery of products or services.

Each business has a pattern of sales. Some maintain a fairly constant sales volume; others rise and dip with seasonal or holiday demands or for other reasons.

Your markets need your products and services most during the peak seasons, when demand is greatest. If you cannot meet their demands, they may lose their season. Therefore, timing is an important element of sales.

If a clothing manufacturer needs textiles in May to fill orders in June, it cannot wait until August. If clothing retailers need garments in September, they cannot wait until December. If you cannot deliver your products on time, your customers will cancel their orders and look for more reliable suppliers.

Timing is important in other ways too. If a new housing development is undertaken in Madison, Wisconsin, the consumers who purchase the homes will need all kinds of home furnishings, bathroom and kitchen items, maintenance and cleaning products, and so on.

If your marketing function, in researching different business areas, learns of the new development and potential demand, it can seek to identify product markets and customers in the Madison business area. If your products are related in any way to homemaking, furnishing, gardening, or home appliances, the timing is right for launching a concentrated sales campaign in the Madison area.

The marketing department must keep in tune with the times. Changes are constantly going on in markets, lifestyles, and preferences. For years golf was the big game; now tennis has become a prime sport. Those businesses which sell products or services related in any way to tennis have potentials to benefit from the increased interest in this sport—if their marketing functions act in time and research the potentials in that growing market area.

Selling costs money. Shipping, salespersons, sales offices or showrooms, and car expenses all add to your costs. Where such expenses are higher than justified by revenues, the business may use other means—distributors, wholesalers, sales representatives, or agents—

to help it get its products and services to the right place at the right time.

Sometimes a business cannot profitably sell in certain business areas, because of seasonal demand or because sales potentials are not strong enough to cover the costs of the sales. In other cases, businesses in certain business areas buy in such small quantities at a time that shipping costs eat up any profit. In still other cases, business areas may cover a large territory, as in some mountain states in the United States, where small populations are spread out over a large area.

Possibly your customers need immediate and fast supply, and it may take too long for you to ship your products or deliver your services in business areas far from the location of your business. Ordinarily under such circumstances, one might meet such demand by establishing a warehouse; however, this may prove too costly to be offset by sales in certain business areas. Yet, the sales potential in these areas may be such that you cannot afford to ignore them. In all such cases, using distributors, wholesalers, or agents may be the answer.

Distributors, wholesalers, manufacturers' agents, sales representatives, and others work with businesses to help them reach product markets which for many reasons the business itself cannot or does not want to serve directly.

Because it is important for a business to know its market composition in different product markets as well as the effects of changes in the product markets and market composition of its customers, those businesses which are close to the product markets and aware of trends and changes are best equipped to reach them. If a business in New York City, for instance, wants to sell products or services in San Francisco, it would have to make a complete study of the product markets and market areas and the kinds of customers in that area. It would also have to know the demand and buying power of those markets and the changes that may affect them.

On the other hand, if there is a business in San Francisco that already sells to the same product markets and has made that marketing study, it might act as the agent for your business and sell your products and services along with its own.

Distributors, wholesalers, manufacturers' agents, and sales representatives use their knowledge of product markets and of customers within those markets to help you sell your products or services without having to send in your own salespersons, establish your own warehouse, or ship long-distance to individual customers. For this service they receive commissions on sales, special discounts, or combinations of various manners of payment.

A wholesaler may purchase your products and services in large

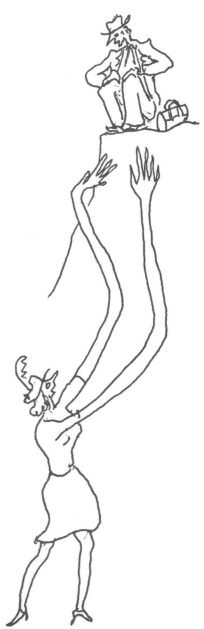

Stretch your product markets by working through distributors, wholesalers, and agents.

quantities, or on special orders, for discounted prices (less than you charge your customers). Your business ships the goods to the wholesaler, with the shipping costs figured in the discounted price. The wholesaler sells those products and services to the product markets in its business area, collects payment (costs plus profit), takes care of its own shipping to customers, its own sales force, its own warehousing, and so on. Thus, your products and services are sold in the distant business area without your having to become directly involved.

Alternatively, a distributor may take orders for the purchase of your products or services from customers in your product markets in distant business areas and send those orders to your business to be filled. In this case you ship the products and services to the customers, bill them and collect payments, and pay a commission (a percentage of sales) to the distributor for its work. Again, you sell to distant product markets without becoming directly involved in selling.

A manufacturers' agent may sell the products of many businesses that fall into the same product markets (though not necessarily into the same market areas or levels). The agent will sell your products and services to customers and send you the orders to be filled. Like the distributors, agents earn a commission for their work.

Sometimes distributors, wholesalers, or agents work on a consignment basis. That means they actually receive quantities of your products from your business but pay for them—less discounts or commissions—only after they sell them. Whatever cannot be sold is returned to you. Other distributors may buy your products and services at a discounted price and sell them to local wholesalers at a smaller discount. The local wholesalers then sell them to the customers in the product market.

In whatever formula or combination, businesses often benefit in such transactions because they can sell to more markets and thereby increase their sales and profits. If they had to pay for their own salespersons, warehouses, market studies, and so on, the costs might prevent them from dealing with those far-away markets. In effect, they save those costs and use part of the savings to pay agents in the form of commissions or discounts.

Distributors, wholesalers, and agents must be familiar with the product markets to which you want to sell. They must have identified actual product markets that meet your conditions, and they must have the staff and facilities to properly serve your business and your customers. Furthermore, if they buy your products and services themselves for resale, they must meet your conditions to qualify as customers themselves.

If your business sold leather products, you would be ill-advised to use an agent that deals in product markets for metal products. You must pick your agents, wholesalers, and distributors carefully. If they do not sell in the business areas you are trying to reach, you do not sell. And if they cannot get the products or services to where the demand and buying power are, then all of your research, planning, and advertising is lost.

When your name is on the product, the final or intermediate customer blames your business for any problems, even though they may be caused by your agents. This is another good reason to pick your agents carefully; you must be able to trust them to carry out your business as conscientiously as you would.

Businesses must sell their products and services for the right price.

The right price for your business is one that enables you to recover all costs and earn a profit. At the same time, it must allow you to sell enough products and services to meet your operational needs.

The right price to the customer is the lowest price for the kind of products or services, their quality, material, delivery, and sales terms and conditions. In addition, the price must be such that it enables the customer to sell enough products or services to its own markets to meet its own operational needs.

You must remember that your costs are also determined by delivery schedules and expenses, the period of time you must wait for payment, and the size of the purchase. Customers are equally concerned about payment periods, discounts for prompt payment, delivery schedules, and sufficient supply on demand. And both you and your customers will usually be concerned with the stability of prices, because fixed price levels are essential for planning and budgeting.

Neither you nor your customer should enter into a transaction that will cause either to lose money. You must determine the lowest price that still allows you a reasonable profit, and unless you are able to reduce your costs further, any sale below that limit must be turned down.

The right pricing can only be found through research. You must determine all your costs, including taxes and commissions, and the price you set must be sufficient to recover those costs and earn a profit.

Through its accounting systems (discussed in the next chapter), a business keeps track of all its costs. These include costs for its facilities, its equipment, its machinery, its labor, its fuel and power, its professionals, its management, its shipping costs, its sales costs, its tax needs, and its financing costs—in other words, all its costs in factor markets. When all these costs have been added together, manage-

Businesses must sell their products or services for the right price. What is the right price?

What is the right price for your business and for your customers?

ment has an accurate picture of the actual costs for producing, processing, handling, fabricating, or delivering—whatever the case may be—its products or services. *The sales price must include all costs plus a profit margin.*

A business must know its product markets and their composition and buying power.

If no one wants to buy your products or services, it makes no difference what price you establish. If someone is interested in buying your products or services, but the interest is not strong, then that potential customer may not be sufficiently motivated to pay the price you ask. On the other hand, if people want your products or services badly enough, they may be willing to meet your price even if they consider it too high.

The laws of supply and demand relate directly to prices and to their acceptance or rejection by your customers. If you were the only business selling certain products or services, all customers would have to come to you. If they wanted those products or services badly enough, they might pay any price. If, on the other hand, you were only one of a hundred businesses selling the same products or services, customers would look for the best buy and you would have to compete for sales. That is the way it is in business.

A business must know its competition.

You must know how many other businesses offer the same or similar products or services to customers in your product markets. If you seek to capture a sufficient share of the total markets, the prices that you establish for your goods and services cannot be higher than the prices your competitors charge for products and services of similar quality. To charge higher prices than the competition, you must offer some additional value, or you will lose sales.

If you sell products and services in demand by customers and have few competitors, the demand may be so strong that the supply cannot meet it. In that case, the prices charged by you and your competition can rise with little customer resistance. On the other hand, if the supply is more than ample, cutomer resistance to higher prices may force you to meet the lowest prices of your competition.

By the same token, if the demand by the customers of your customers dropped, the laws of supply and demand would again apply. Therefore, anything that affects your product markets and their demand can affect the willingness of your customers to pay your prices.

A business must be concerned not only with the customers' interest

to buy, but also with their ability to do so—that is, with their buying power.

Customers may want your products or services, and even need them, but they must have the money to pay for them. Suppose that consumers in your product markets want to buy your products or services, but because of high unemployment in the area, many of them cannot afford to buy from you now. This would mean that although there is a strong interest for your product, the *actual* demand, because of the lack of buying power of your customers, is quite low. The few customers who can afford to buy your kind of products would have to be distributed among your business and its competitors; therefore, the actual market would be small, the competition high, and prices would have a tendency to drop.

The actual demand for your products and services will depend on the willingness of potential customers to buy your products and services at your prices, and on their ability to pay for them. Therefore, you must concern yourself with market buying power and with the disposable incomes and the spending patterns of consumers.

Through research, businesses can study the market composition of their product markets and examine the availability of money for purchases. They can identify the kinds of purchases made with available money and the amounts, in quantity and dollars, of those purchases.

If your business sells kitchen appliances and research indicates that consumers have less money available and are spending less for kitchen appliances, that information tells you that your actual product markets have diminished. In all likelihood, consumers will be offered various deals by appliance dealers to generate sales. Competition is bound to increase, and prices will probably fall.

Your markets may demand your products or services but have no money to buy them.

Marketing also means justifying the prices you get for your products or services.

If the quality of your products or services is poor and the materials are cheap, or you employ unskilled or untrained labor, it is difficult to justify charging the same price as competitors do for quality goods or services.

In competing, each business must try to convince customers that its products or services deserve the prices set because of their quality, materials, design, usefulness, strength, or special characteristics or benefits. Each business may push different features, one, the usefulness and strength of its products, and another, their design and quality.

When a business advertises or sells its product or service, it should promote those features that have been found to be most appealing and most demanded. For instance, when demand for small cars increased, the dealers pushed the small size of their cars. Similarly, when cars with gas-saving features were in demand, the dealers were quick to emphasize the low fuel consumption of their models.

Businesses must study the prices charged by their competitors.

You must study the prices, products, and services of your competitors. If they are giving more than you for the same price, you may lose sales. On the other hand, if they are giving less than you, you may gain sales, but you must make that difference known to customers.

When competitors charge less for products or services of the same quality, you must consider ways to reduce your prices without hurting the business. *However, remember that you must still recover costs and earn profits.*

Some ways to reduce costs are: buy better in your factor markets, substitute materials where they do not affect the prime features of your product or service, reduce production or handling costs by increasing efficiency, consider mechanizing manual operations, use less expensive packaging when possible. These methods will be discussed at length in the next section of this chapter.

The marketing function determines whether a business can compete, how it can compete, how much it can charge for products or services, how strong the demand is for products or services of the business, how great the buying power of different product markets is, how consumers spend their money, and whether the supply of your products or services is greater or less than the demand for them.

As it finds out all those things, the marketing department must inform management of any changes that affect the business so that management can respond to them to insure a good business balance.

Production

Just as there are many kinds of businesses in many different fields, the number of functions and the number of employees and outside professionals involved in a business operation can vary widely. One person may be doing everything, or many thousands of persons may perform many different functions each.

Top management is faced with two prime problems. One, it must be able to control its business through effective chains of command and communication and reporting systems. Two, it must be able to pinpoint costs so that it can make modifications necessary to respond to changes inside or outside the business.

To be able to determine costs, top management, with its accounting functions assisting it, breaks down all functions in the business, including outside professionals, and groups them according to their contribution to the business process. In this way, it can evaluate reports and accounts, compute costs for different groups of functions, and cut, add, or modify functional groups in response to changes. In other words, breaking down activities within the organization into functional groups helps top management insure a sound business balance and profitable operations.

For such purposes of control, small businesses generally can be broken down into four basic functional divisions, which represent distinct functional areas within the total operation. Each functional area has costs and staffing requirements that distinguish it from the other functional areas, and each can be studied, changed, or modified separately. On the other hand, although each contributes in different ways to the success of the business, it is directly related to the others in the business process.

Those divisions are administration, production, sales, and accounting/finance. Marketing and research can fall into either the sales or the top-management division.

Administration includes top management, planning, and modification. *Production* includes purchasing, receiving and shipping, inventorying, processing (handling, assembling, producing, fabricating, packaging, organizing, and so on), record maintenance, and management of facilities, equipment, machinery, and tools used in production.

Sales includes actual selling, sales strategy development, promotion, advertising (in conjunction with marketing), reporting, and record maintenance. *Accounting/finance* includes the servicing of all receivables (money owed to the business) and payables (money owed by the business), maintenance of records and accounts, payroll maintenance, cost accounting breakdowns, and tax records and payments. Personnel services (hiring, firing, insurance and benefits management) may be part of either the administrative or the accounting/finance function, depending on the size of staffs.

All functional areas have managers, and all of them must report through chains of command to top management. Top management (administration) makes the final decisions, based on reports and recommendations of the division managers and of managers within the functional divisions.

Thus, production is a separate functional division, and it has a functional division manager representing top management, besides other managers in functional groups and functions within the division.

The prime responsibility of the production manager is to meet the production goals set by top management, which were developed in cooperation with the production manager and the rest of the management team.

The production manager assists top management in planning and defines the limitations of production so that top management can set realistic goals. He or she is responsible for the performance and productivity of all the workers and managers in the division and for the fulfillment of all functions necessary to meet the established goals.

The production manager also has a responsibility as part of the management team.

Production managers must work with top management and other divisional managers to gather data and information about internal operations and outside conditions that bear on the business, and make such data and information known to top management. They must maintain the records and reporting of the division to insure that the chains of communication and control are open and working for the good of the business.

Although many schools of business do not recognize a production division for every kind of business, it is advisable to do so. Every business has many functions, and each has to be monitored for costs, productivity, and value to the business. Grouping those functions that deal with certain aspects of doing something to products or services into a production division makes it easier to monitor and evaluate the total operations. Thus, although retailers, wholesalers, distributors, and service businesses may not produce in the same sense as manufacturers, many functions in their operations involve labor and materials in similar ways as manufacturing.

In retail operations, certain functions call for purchasing of products and services, receiving and inventorying of supplies, unpacking and marking, packaging and shipping, handling products and services, filling containers, maintaining records of supplies received or sales delivered, and so on. Each of those functions represents work to be performed by labor, whether it is the labor of employees or of the owner of the business. That labor takes time, and no matter who performs it, that person must be paid in some way. In that sense, all the functions mentioned in our retail example are concerned with production and therefore belong in the production division. And the same holds true for service businesses.

In a manufacturing situation, the direct use of labor and materials to produce, fabricate, assemble, and process products becomes more obvious, and grouping of such functions into production divisions is more broadly accepted or understood.

Production managers wear two hats. They manage their production division and at the same time are members of the management team.

Whether a business is small or large, it incurs costs for the handling and processing of its materials, goods, or services, and those costs can be better identified and estimated by grouping certain functions into production.

If a person in a business is responsible for sales as well as production, then that person is both sales manager and production manager and must assume the duties and responsibilities of two divisions. Divisions are groups of functions that can be separately monitored and evaluated to measure their costs and value to the business.

LABOR

In determining the costs of its production division, large or small, top management breaks them down into costs for materials, labor, and overhead (indirect factory expenses).

All labor and materials used to process products or deliver services fall into production, as do all managers involved in the production process—except the production manager, who is also part of top management and whose cost is therefore charged to the administration division.

MATERIALS

All supplies, fuel, power, and maintenance and service for all machinery and equipment used in processing or handling are part of the production costs, as are depreciation on machinery and equipment or tools and expenses for facilities used in production. Finally, all labor, such as secretaries or clerks, that is not directly involved in processing of materials or handling of products or services but works for the production division must be included in the production costs as overhead.

All of those costs are grouped into three different categories—labor, materials, and overhead—for two reasons. One, this makes it easier to maintain accounting records and compute the costs of the production division. Two, the costs for different kinds of labor, materials, and management are subject to different conditions and affect total production costs in different ways.

OPERATIONS

In simple terms, all costs for labor employed to perform functions that are directly related to the production process (handling, assembling, fabricating, receiving, shipping, and so on) are counted as *labor costs of production*.

All costs for materials and intermediate products and services used in the processing of the products or services of the business are counted as *materials costs* of the production division.

Any costs for personnel, office workers, or professionals not directly involved in processing the products of the business but employed in the production division are *overhead costs* of production (indirect factory expenses). This category also includes all costs of supplies, facilities, power, fuel, telephones, water, and depreciation of machinery, equipment, vehicles, or tools used for production.

INCLUDING OVERHEAD

Production costs

Production planning and operations start only after other divisions have conducted research, developed plans and strategies, and studied costs.

Before it begins production of its products or services, the business must first know a number of things. It must be informed about its product markets; its business areas; the market areas and levels it will sell to; the market demand for products and services of the kind it seeks to sell; the market buying power for such goods or services; the money available in its product markets to buy its products or services; the interest and priorities of customers in its product markets; the products and services of its competitors and their price structures; and the number of competitors.

It must know what designs, materials, sizes, and colors its potential customers prefer and the prices they are willing to pay for products and services of different quality.

It must know whether or not it can get the supplies it needs in factor markets to fill its production needs, and what the current and expected prices of those supplies are. It must have studied the economic indicators for its own industry and the industries to which its customers belong. It must know all it can about the customers of its potential customers, including the factors that may affect their interest and buying power.

It must estimate the share of markets it can expect and the costs of producing its products or services. Finally, if it finds that it lacks the financial resources to buy the factor inputs it needs to meet its goals, it must determine whether or not it can borrow more money.

Before planning production, then, top management must do its homework. *No business can gamble. It must have the facts to make sound business judgments.*

Once top management has done its research, it sits down with the production manager to decide what it is capable of doing, how much it will cost, and how much it can produce with the financial and other resources it has at its disposal. It must review the kinds of materials it must use and the supply and costs of other factor inputs it needs to meet its production goals.

These meetings of top management with the production managers must be held on a regular basis, no matter whether the business is starting fresh or has been operating successfully for a number of years. You must constantly go over the costs, resources, and limitations of production that can affect current and future operations. If your business is small and managers act as division managers for several different functional divisions, you will still have to hold the same meetings, and they must cover the same ground.

Through planning and analysis of costs, resources, and limitations on productivity or supply, top management can determine the quantity of products and services it can produce at a given time, and the price levels at which it can afford to sell them.

Every business, as we have seen, must sell its products and services at prices that recover all costs and earn profits after costs. Its profit margin—the profit after costs—is determined by comparing total sales with total costs.

If a business manufactures typewriters and produces 1,000 typewriters a year at a total cost for its entire operation, including all functional divisions, of $1 million, each typewriter would cost it an average of $1,000 to produce. To recover all costs and make a profit, it would have to sell the typewriters for more than $1,000 each. If typewriters of the same quality were sold by other manufacturers for $500 each, that price would clearly be too high to meet competition. If, on the other hand, it sold the typewriters for less than $1,000, it would lose money.

Two things play a part in determining costs. One is the cost of the production division alone, the other, the overall cost of all the other divisions.

Once top management and the production manager set certain goals and budget the costs for producing a certain number of products or services, the production manager must seek to achieve those goals and stay within the established cost limits, as must the managers of all the other divisions. Obviously, if production does not reach its goals and produces less for the budgeted costs, or produces the same amount for greater costs, then cost estimates are thrown out of line and the plans of the business are upset. Similarly, if the quality of the final products or services fails to meet the established standards, the competitive position of the business may be endangered.

The same holds true for other functions. All functions of the business are concerned with the performance of certain work in different operational areas; although their performance may not be measured as easily, they must strive to meet the goals set for them.

In determining the overall costs of products and services, the failure of any functional division to achieve its goals can affect the costs of producing products or services.

The failure of any one of the functional divisions to meet its goals can increase overall costs.

If management planned to produce 1,000 typewriters at a total cost of $200 each, and all functional divisions except one met their cost goals, the failure of that one division to stay within budget could affect overall costs. For instance, if each division were allocated $40,000 and there were five divisions in the total operation, the budgeted costs for producing 1,000 typewriters at an overall cost of $200 each would be $200,000. If the cost of one division rose to $60,000, the overall costs would be $220,000, and the cost for each of the 1,000 typewriters would be $220.

The costs of the production division alone are the costs for materials, labor, and overhead as previously described.

If the production division spent $100,000 for materials, labor, and overhead, and it produced 1,000 typewriters, the production costs for each typewriter would be $100. The overall costs to the business for the manufacture and sale of those same 1,000 typewriters may be $200,000, because of the costs of other functional divisions in the operations.

Sometimes costs can be affected by outside factors and conditions.

Even if all divisions are operating soundly, with each meeting its cost goals, changes outside the business may cause its overall costs to rise. If taxes are raised, for instance, costs will go up. If the prices of supplies, rental, or fuel or power rise, this will affect costs. If labor wage scales rise, costs will go up for employees. Such increases, which are more often than not outside the control of the business, must be incorporated in its revised cost calculations.

Changes in sales may also affect production costs.

When computing production costs, management adds up all the costs in the production division that relate to its materials, labor, and overhead. For that total cost, production is to meet its goals and produce a certain quantity of products and services, which are sold at a price that will enable the business to recover its overall costs and earn a profit.

If sales increase, production will be called upon by management to produce more products or services to fill the increased orders. To meet the increased needs, production's costs for labor, materials, and overhead will rise. Those increased costs, which are tied to sales, are called *variable costs*. If the sales of the products or services of the business dropped, production may be called upon by management to produce less. In that case, the production division may use less materials and less labor, and incur less overhead. Again, that reduction in costs is tied to sales and therefore counted as variable costs.

Other costs of the production division are not tied to sales. For instance, whether or not sales go up or down, the division still needs machinery, facilities, and a certain minimum number of workers and managers. Costs for items that do not vary with sales are called *fixed costs.*

In computing the costs of the production division and of the products and services it produces, both variable and fixed costs must be included.

If a business plans for the production of its products and services against estimated sales of those products and services to its customers, it must keep in mind that sales may go up or down at any time for many reasons, as discussed in the section on product markets in Chapter 3. These variations in sales could cause changes in the variable costs of the business.

Management must allow in its budgets for such variations and set aside the financial and other resources to meet increased costs. In the same way, if sales dropped, the variable costs of the production division may decrease, and management must be prepared for this possibility.

Fixed costs, as we said, do not change with sales. Therefore, if the production division has too many fixed and too few variable costs, then it cannot reduce its costs significantly if sales drop. Under such circumstances, the costs for producing fewer products and services may be almost as high as those for producing more of them, which means that the cost per item produced rises.

The greater the percentage of fixed costs to total costs of the production division, the less able it is to vary costs when sales go down. Therefore, to be able to respond to changes in sales, the business must maximize its variable costs.

The greater the number of fixed costs is, the harder it is for adjustments in total costs to restore the business balance.

If a business rents a facility for production when sales are high, the rental for that facility may not cost much if measured against total sales and production costs. If sales drop and only half the space is needed to meet the revised production goals, the business may be able to move to smaller and cheaper space when its lease has expired. But if the business owns the facility, it may not be able to sell it when sales go down and therefore may be forced to operate in space that has become too big and too expensive. In that case, the high level of the fixed costs for the building it owns and occupies will cut into profits.

All functional divisions have fixed and variable costs. However, while costs in other divisions may vary for a multitude of reasons, those of the production division can vary only with the quantity of products or services produced. This is because the costs of producing certain amounts of products and services were established in plan-

Your break-even point is reached when total sales in dollars equal total overall costs of the entire business operation.

ning, with every need accounted for. Those needs only change as sales levels, and hence production goals, change.

When management has determined its fixed and variable costs, it can compute its *break-even point*. The break-even point is that point where the total dollar value of all sales equals the overall costs of the business.

The break-even point tells management at what sales level the business will recover all costs without any profits. It tells management the minimum amount of sales necessary for the business not to lose any money.

Although the actual calculation of the break-even point will not be discussed here, management should know that for any business, it is largely determined by the relative amount of fixed and variable costs that it has. If most of the costs of the business are variable (that is, change with sales levels), the business will have a low break-even point since in this case costs are largely determined by sales and low sales will mean low total operating costs. If, on the other hand, most of the costs of a business are fixed, it will have a high break-even point since it will need a high level of sales to recover these costs. Thus, each business will have its own break-even point depending on how many of its costs are fixed and how many are variable. Management must know the business's break-even point in order to establish minimum sales goals.

In production, costs are computed on *unit cost,* or the cost of producing one product item or one unit of service.

Unit costs can be viewed in two ways. One, the cost of each unit may be measured in terms of *overall costs* for the entire business operation. Alternatively, the unit cost for producing the product or service may be based on the costs of the *production division* alone.

If the overall operational costs of producing a pen are $1, the same pen might cost $.50 in terms of the production division alone. In determining unit costs for the production division alone, only the costs charged to that division are of course counted.

The two means of computing unit costs are important, because costs in the production division can generally be varied much less than those in other functional divisions. Because of this relative inflexibility of production costs, the cost of other divisions very often have to be reduced to a greater degree if necessary to restore a sound business balance and keep sales prices competitive.

Management must look at many places to modify operations, but it must know where to look and how to modify operations and costs without hurting the business.

Management must look at many places in the operations of the business to modify functions and save on costs.

Our observations about fixed and variable costs are true not only for manufacturing operations, which have a clear-cut production division, but for all businesses, including retail, wholesale, and service businesses. They, too, have divisions that are concerned with production—though less obviously so—and costs in those divisions are tied to sales, that is, are variable.

If a retail business, for instance, needs two men to unload shipments, carry them to its stockroom, unpack them, mark and tag them, place them on shelves in sales areas, package goods, and make deliveries, then it has costs tied to sales. If sales drop, it may not need two men to do the work; therefore, the costs for that labor are *variable costs*. If the business occupies a large store, and the rental cost for that facility cannot be reduced when sales drop, this is a *fixed cost* of the business. Also, if sales drop, less wrapping paper and fewer bags will be needed; therefore, the costs for the paper and bags are again *variable costs*.

Similarly, if a wholesaler rents trucks for delivery of its products to customers and sales drop, it may need fewer trucks. Clearly then, the cost of renting trucks is a *variable cost*. The unit cost per case of products that the wholesaler ships or delivers would be determined by the costs of labor and trucks and marking and handling in its warehouse. In some instances, the number of stops that a truck makes to deliver goods can be translated into unit costs per customer for delivery. If sales drop and fewer stops are made, a truck may still be needed. The truck is a fixed cost, then, because it is needed whether sales go up or down. If sales decrease, it may still cost the same to run the truck, but since it now makes fewer deliveries, each delivery costs more.

Controlling Production Costs

Management must regularly measure its actual production costs and compare them to cost estimates in budgets. If it has done its job, it knows its fixed and variable costs in its production division. It knows that the variable costs vary only with sales.

For the production division, the costs to be considered relate not only to production proper but also to purchasing, inventorying, shipping, record-keeping, and quality control. Each of these functions must be properly controlled so that the business can achieve its goals for the lowest possible cost without sacrificing efficiency or quality.

First, the production manager must break down every function in the production division that is necessary to meet the goals set by management. The costs for staffing, supplies, facilities, fuel, power, and machinery or equipment must be estimated and measured as production goes on.

For instance, if an operation called for cutting metal sheets to

In production, every penny counts. Each penny saved means a better competitive position in your product markets.

size, it would take so many workers and certain cutting machinery, tools and knives, power to run the machines, and supplies to fulfill that function. The production manager can estimate the costs for those items, including the depreciation on the machines and the equipment. Similarly, the production manager would have to estimate the time it takes to cut the metal to size per unit, the amount of metal sheet to be cut, and the amount wasted if some of the material is trimmed and discarded. In other words, the cost of the metal sheets both before and after it is cut to size must be figured.

In this way, every function within the production division is identified, evaluated, and measured for labor, materials, and overhead costs.

Often cost savings can be achieved by eliminating unnecessary functions or by merging similar ones to reduce labor, production time, or handling. Clearly, the more handling or processing of materials there is, the more labor, time, machinery and equipment, and other inputs are needed, and each costs money. The production manager must try to minimize handling or processing so as to save costs.

In production, time is money. If operations are not properly balanced so that work flows from operation to operation without loss of time, production costs will be unnecessarily high. By the same token, the longer completed products or services remain in the facility without being shipped, the higher the production costs. And if materials or supplies are not on hand when they are needed, this will again raise production costs.

If the production goal for a particular operation calls for workers to process 100 items each per hour, and for various reasons, they actually process no more than 50 items per hour while being paid the same wages and using the same inputs, such as fuel or power, then the costs for that operation have increased substantially. Perhaps time is wasted moving work in progress (parts or partially assembled products) from operation to operation because of the distance between different production units. The production manager must make sure that materials, parts, and work in progress are moved at the fastest possible rate so that the costs of labor for each load moved are kept to a minimum.

If machines or workers are idle because certain materials have not arrived or the work in an earlier operation has not been completed or parts have not been moved to a new operation, that loss of time can only increase production costs. Also, if there are not enough workers in an operation, causing it to move too slowly, this might hold up later operations. Again, time will be wasted, and costs will increase.

Products stored in a shipping room for a length of time without being shipped cannot be charged to customers as sales until they have actually been delivered, and the business cannot expect pay-

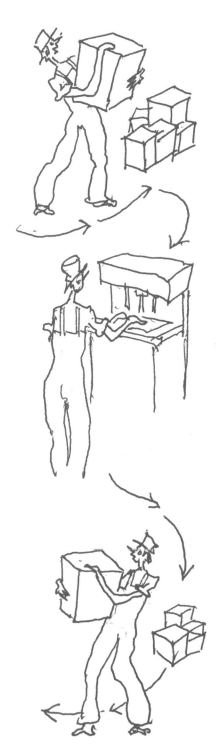

Production must maintain a steady flow of materials.

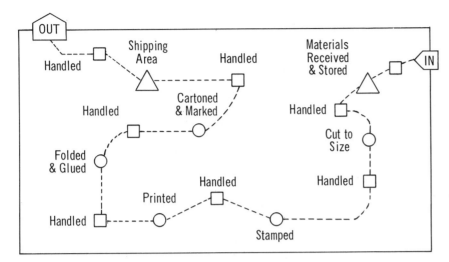

Figure 6(a). Flowchart of a manufacturing operation.

ment for them. If the goods had been shipped, payment could have come sooner, and that money could have been used to pay for the production of more products and services. Products tied up in inventory lose money and raise production costs.

The production manager must chart the flow of work through the facility, from operation to operation, to identify all necessary steps, determine what labor will be needed, reduce handling and time losses, and insure steady work flow. Production planning is the key to controlling costs.

A manufacturing flow chart may look like Figure 6(a); and a typical flow chart for a retail operation is shown in Figure 6(b).

As these figures illustrate, each kind of business handles products and services, uses various inputs in its operations, and requires

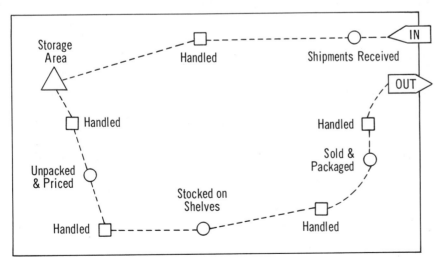

Figure 6(b). Flowchart of a retail operation.

○ Operation   □ Moved from place to place   △ Storage

labor. Each operation takes an amount of time that can be estimated by the production manager, and in each case, increased sales will demand increased production that must be allowed for in planning.

If a retail store, for instance, sold products in great quantities but did not have enough labor in its packaging and check-out counter, a bottleneck would develop and customers would get irritated and hostile. We have probably all experienced this sometimes at supermarkets. Therefore, if the store did not allow for enough salespersons to take care of customers, it would lose sales. On the other hand, if it had too many salespersons for its sales, it would incur excessive production costs.

The amount of work that can be produced in a given time is a prime consideration of the production manager. Called the time-cost factor, it establishes the needs for labor and determines how materials move from operation to operation.

Time loss can sharply upset production estimates. Management must constantly check to make sure that nothing is holding up the flow of materials or work in process and that each production unit performs its functions in the most efficient way.

The production manager must also make sure that all the inputs purchased in factor markets are available when needed, received on schedule, of the quality needed and ordered, and in supply as long as they are needed. The prices of such purchases must be checked continuously to meet established goals and where possible, reduce costs.

The conditions and problems in factor markets have already been discussed in depth. A business must buy right, be assured of ample supply, and get supplies when they are needed. The costs of the products or services it buys must be competitive and be monitored on a regular basis. Also, as we have seen, it is always good to have more than one supplier, if possible, of your needs. Dependence on a single source of supply can be risky; if anything happens to that source, you may be left without supplies.

The *purchasing function* in the production division handles this aspect of the business. It must identify the right sources and the right products and services at the right price, keeping alert to special discounts and bulk purchases, and it must work constantly to insure ample supply as and when needed to meet production goals.

The purchasing function must also keep abreast of new materials, products and services, and their sources, as well as new technology affecting the industry to which the business belongs. And it must coordinate all purchases with the production manager to ensure that there will be no interruptions of supplies.

To ensure a steady flow of inputs when they are needed, the production division may buy more than it needs at a given time so that it will be ahead of purchases if something interrupts the scheduled delivery of inputs.

The materials, products, or services that production purchases as a safeguard against the interruption of deliveries are *inventory*. Unless shortages of supply are expected, the inventory of factor inputs should never be too far ahead of production needs, because once inventory has been purchased, the price for those factor inputs is fixed. If the prices of any of the inputs bought in factor markets drop, then the materials or products stored as inventory may have cost more than current market prices, and the opportunity to reduce costs through buying right may be lost until the inventory is used up.

However, sometimes it works the other way around: The costs of new inputs may rise to higher prices than your business paid for the goods it has in inventory. In that case, buying inventory ahead of production needs would save costs, namely the difference between the old and the new prices of the purchased goods.

To inventory properly, the production manager must work closely with the purchasing and marketing functions to anticipate price changes, shortages, and business interruptions of suppliers.

Sometimes a production division inventories *work in process*—parts of products and partially completed or assembled goods—which may be used as components for more than one product or service. This is done to provide some flexibility in response to varying sales of different products. This kind of inventory must be carefully monitored because the demand for certain products or services can fall and sales can drop. If this happens, it may take too long to reduce that inventory, and this would raise costs.

Similarly, should a product line suddenly become undesirable and sales fall off completely, *finished goods* stored may be useless. As unprocessed materials or semifinished products, they might be used for the production of new products; once assembled or processed, however, they lose value unless they can be reused in production.

Production is concerned not only about buying right but also about shipping in the most efficient way.

Products and services must flow to customers as promised in sales contracts. Customers need products and services to fill their customers' needs and to respond to seasonal demands and deadlines. If a customer receives winter-apparel products too late for the season, its customers will not buy them.

The responsibility for this side of the business lies with the *shipping function,* which must find the best ways to deliver the products and services to customers at the least cost.

Shipping costs are generally charged to the customer, and if not, they are usually built into the price. In either case, it is in the interest not only of your customer but of your own business to keep these costs at a minimum. The shipping function must identify the best routes for shipping and compare the prices and quality of service of different shippers. Depending on markets, air freight, trucking firms, railroads, or ships may be used. Each of these has its advantages and disadvantages.

Air freight may get your products delivered faster, but costs are generally higher. Trucks may get your products delivered fast and reach out-of-the-way places that have no airports or railroad stations. Railroads may be cheaper for heavy or bulky products that might pose problems for trucks and planes.

The ways in which products are packaged, their size and weight, and their value, as well as time and money constraints on deliveries, determine the choice of the freight carrier. The shipping function must check with different kinds of carriers to determine variations in costs, the kinds of services they offer, and the places they can reach efficiently.

The production division must furthermore maintain accurate records.

Pennies are important in production; they can make the difference between meeting and not meeting production goals. If the costs of production rise above estimates, then the profit margin, which was added to sales prices, will be lost.

Each function and operation must be constantly monitored, and accurate records must be kept of all purchases and inventories; of the amount of materials or goods processed in each operation; of the time it took to process them; of the shipping costs; of the costs of handling and moving work in process; and of the costs of all factor inputs and of the facility itself.

The production division must respond immediately to changes in sales and try to avoid loss or waste. To accomplish this, the production manager must meet with the top-management team to review sales and competitive products or services and their prices. At the same time, top management must be kept informed of production volumes and costs and of differences, if any, between actual and projected volumes and costs. This requires regular—often even daily—reports to top management.

The production manager must be concerned with maintaining constant levels of quality for all products or services.

All production divisions must have a *quality control function* to ensure that the products or services produced maintain the levels of quality desired by customers and match the samples offered by salespersons when the sales were made.

The customers and users of your products and services must be able to depend on their having a uniform quality. If they are used as component parts of other products, the quality of those products is only as good as that of your component part. If that part is poorly manufactured or irregular, it may cause the other product to fail or become undesirable in its markets.

A business can only keep its customers if it supplies them with uniform, quality products as represented at the time of sale. Loss of confidence in your product or service by your customers can mean the loss of sales to them. The quality-control function inspects workmanship, performance, quality of materials used, and uniformity of products as compared to the original specifications set by management. It must work closely with the production manager to insure uniformity of quality and to make such modifications as necessary to restore the desired quality level.

When all the costs for purchasing, processing and handling, receiving and shipping, inventorying, record-keeping, and quality control have been identified by the production manager, top management can calculate the *unit costs of production*. To these must be added the costs of all other divisions to arrive at the *total* unit cost of your products. For the business to break even, the sales price per item must be sufficient to recover that total unit cost, and enough units must be sold to cover fixed costs. Anything above the costs of all functions in all divisions can be considered your *profit margin*.

Profit margins must be tailored to market demand, acceptance by customers, and competition.

The combination of fixed and variable costs and the sales price determines your break-even point. If your sales prices did not recover those costs, you obviously would lose money. Therefore, your break-even point establishes a fixed lower limit on your prices. However, nobody is in business just to recover costs; you must make a profit as well.

Profit margins, unlike your costs (assuming that you have kept them to the minimum), are flexible and must be established by considering the situation in your markets. You must know how much the competition charges for comparable products, and you must also make sure that your customers are able and willing to pay the prices you ask.

Even if you are the only manufacturer of a product that is in high demand, the prices you set must be within reach of the individuals or organizations that you have identified as potential customers. If they

Net profit is profit after taxes.

The customer may rarely see you or your facility. Your salesperson becomes the image of your business— for better or worse.

refuse to pay your prices, your products will sit idly in your warehouses. And of course, customer resistance to high prices for your products will be even greater if there is strong competition selling similar products for more attractive prices. Therefore, if your profit margin is too high, you may be unable to sell your products or may have to settle for only a small share of your markets.

High sales at small profits can accomplish the same as lower sales at higher profits.

Costs are costs and profits are profits. Once costs have been recovered, the amount of profit earned per unit can be adjusted as needed. If a company sells 1 million units of its product and earns 10 cents a unit, its profit for all the products sold will be $100,000. If a company sells only 10,000 units of its product and its profit per unit is $10, it also earns $100,000 in profits.

Sales

The sales division represents the business in its product markets, and often the salespersons are the only direct contact the customers have with the business.

To many customers in the product markets, the salesperson *is* the business. Some customers rarely visit the business facility and do not know the top management. All they know about the business is what the salesperson tells them, and their evaluation of the business is only as good as their opinion of the salesperson. Even in retail businesses, customers often deal only with salespersons, not with top management or the sales manager.

The salespersons become the image of the business and of its products and services.

When customers say, "I'll speak to my supplier," they may be talking about your business but thinking about your salesperson. The salesperson becomes the business. This also holds true in many retail situations.

Customers expect salespersons to understand their kind of businesses and their needs. They expect them to be able to discuss the uses of products and services and special features that may be of particular benefit to their business operations.

Salespersons must know their product markets and the market composition. They must be acquainted with the kinds of businesses in that composition and with their special needs and uses of products and services. If they are selling intermediate goods, they must know the ways in which their products can be used in combination with other products and services. They must be informed about the products and services offered by competitors so that they can compare them with their own and explain the relevant differences to their customers.

Salespersons must also be acquainted with the materials used in the products or services, any laws or regulations controlling their use or sale, and important technical details. *If they do not know all those things, they cannot do a good job of selling.*

Salespersons should know about the industries and product markets of their customers and be aware of the demand in different areas of the customers' market composition. They must know the buying power of both their own customers and the customers of their customers.

Salespersons must be familiar with market and economic indicators that affect their customers and the customers of their customers. In this way they can make recommendations to buyers to help them increase their sales and expand their product or service lines. They must be able to help their customers keep abreast of changes in indicators. This builds mutual confidence.

Salespersons must be dependable.

Nothing binds a salesperson and a customer more than confidence on the part of the customer that it can rely on the salesperson to arrange for regular supply, meet delivery schedules, and assist in planning by providing data and information about new or improved products or services, changes in prices, or impending interruptions of supply (strikes, shortages, and so on).

The customer wants to know that once it places an order, it can depend on the salesperson to follow through on it and make sure that it receives the quality it ordered, for the right price and on time. This is true in all kinds of businesses.

Customers must know that the salesperson will call on them on a regular basis and inform them promptly of any changes that may affect the delivery of goods. If they depend on a sales representative to let them know in advance of any strike that will interrupt supplies, that salesperson had better do so. If customers find themselves without supplies because of the salesperson's negligence, they will turn to more reliable suppliers. Often, they may hold orders until the sales representative calls on them.

Salespersons must be sincere and of good character and integrity.

They must never do anything dishonest, underhanded, or sneaky or in any way give customers the impression that they are not nice people to deal with. Once a customer feels it can no longer trust the salesperson, it will look for other suppliers. Also, because they represent the business, the image that the salespersons leave with customers reflects on the image of the business.

Customers are just as smart as salespersons. If they are talked down to, treated without respect, or given inaccurate information, they will doubt the sincerity of the salesperson and look for other suppliers. Just because some dress differently, talk differently, or have trouble expressing themselves, they should be treated with no less respect than other customers. Sincerity shows—and sells.

Salespersons must honestly want to serve their customers.

Salespersons must take an interest in their customers and learn about them, their families, and their problems. They must look at customers as friends and want to help them. Even though a salesperson cannot be friends with all customers, he or she should be friendly to them. Customers do not want to feel that they are not wanted.

Salespersons are dealmakers.

The salesperson tries to make a deal between the business and the customer from which both will benefit. In that role, the salesperson must have some flexibility in pricing and sales terms. That flexibility must be approved by top management first. If the salesperson does not make enough good deals, sales will suffer.

Dealmaking requires a pleasant personality and knowledge of the facts. Also, salespersons must be able to adjust to many different situations and conditions and to different kinds of people.

Salespersons require training, briefing, and preparation.

The *sales manager* of the sales division may be the best salesperson in the world, but unless the salespersons who actually contact and sell to customers are prepared for their jobs, your sales effort will not be successful. That is why this section began with the salespersons who meet with the customers, and not with the sales division, the sales manager, or the business itself. You have to have the right salespersons, and they must be properly trained for their jobs.

The sales manager is in charge of the sales division of the business and is responsible for all of the operations and the performance of that division and its staff. The sales manager is also a member of the management team and works closely with the managers of the other divisions to establish policy, sales goals and strategies, price and sales term limitations, and the degree of flexibility that the sales representatives can be given. Top management has the final word on these matters and is responsible for setting sales goals.

The sales manager works closely with the marketing and research functions to learn about markets, market composition, the kinds and needs of businesses in product markets, the demand in various sectors of the market composition, their buying power, their interest in purchasing the products and services of the business, and their priorities in purchasing. Marketing must also inform the sales manager about the competition—its products and services, prices, quality of products and services, and sales terms.

The sales manager in turn, through the sales force, is able to give the marketing manager important and useful information about the product markets because the salespersons know the customers' reactions to existing products, which may give numerous clues as to how to increase sales.

The sales manager must also work closely with the accounting/finance division to learn about the credit of potential customers, the collection of payments for products or services sold, and other details about customers and their financial condition. If sales collection is slow, the sales force can be of assistance in collecting delinquent payments from customers.

Finally, the sales manager must be in close touch with the production division and the production manager to understand production levels and flow, the scheduling of production and shipments, and the amount of products and services that will be available for sale. He or she must learn about the materials used and their special features and characteristics, the use and potential uses of the products and services, and any technical details and government regulations that could affect sales or the demand for or use of the products or services by customers.

The sales manager is responsible for meeting the sales goals and objectives set by top management, and for establishing specific goals for the salespersons in his or her division. Those goals are accomplished through training, briefings, and preparatory programs for the sales force.

Just as a government would be foolish to send an unprepared or unqualified ambassador to negotiate with another country, so a business would be foolish to send an unprepared or unqualified salesperson to make deals for it with customers and potential customers. Without preparation it will be difficult for salespersons to make deals, and if they do, they may be bad deals for the business.

The sales manager must set up regular training programs to

Your salespersons are the ambassadors you send to make a deal with your customers. Are you happy with the image they project?

prepare sales representatives for their jobs. Only after a salesperson is acquainted with the relevant data and information should he or she be allowed to accompany a trained and experienced salesperson or the sales manager so as to gain experience in meeting with customers.

A business cannot afford to gamble on salespersons. Their success or failure is the success or failure of the business.

Only when the sales manager has tested the abilities of the salespersons and is satisfied that they will be able to represent the business, are knowledgeable, act friendly and sincerely, and are reliable and of good character should they be given their credentials and sent out into the field. The sales division needs qualified salespersons if it is to meet the sales goals set by top management.

The sales manager must supervise sales and contacts in the product markets of the business, study the kinds and number of products and services sold to different sectors of the market composition, help schedule delivery and shipments in conjunction with production, and check with bookkeeping and accounting about credit of customers, collections, and other matters dealing with the division itself.

The sales manager must keep in close touch with the marketing and research functions to identify new opportunities in product markets and develop new product markets. That information must be passed on to the salespersons; they must constantly be briefed on new opportunities and ways to seize them.

Flexibility in prices and sales terms must be used carefully, and only after being cleared with top management.

Although management must be flexible in establishing sales and pricing policies, it must be sure to conform with various federal, state, and local laws that deal with pricing and sales terms and conditions. In some cases, it may be possible to sell large quantities of products or services to one customer. Because of the large volume, the company may be able to reduce its unit sales price to make it more attractive for the buyer to purchase from it rather than other suppliers. In other cases, it may give a large user more time to pay, or it may offer priorities in shipping and delivery to get the large orders. Also, it may offer discounts for certain products and services that are not very much in demand.

The salesperson must be sensitive to the needs of customers and alert to opportunities for large sales. If the salespersons have been briefed on the limits of flexibility, they can respond to opportunities as they develop and make deals on the spot, while interest is still strong. If they have to check each time the situation calls for flexibility, there is a cooling-off period, and the buyer may be offered a better deal by a competitor or change its mind.

A salesperson must try to meet competition for sales.

Most often your business is not the only business offering particular kinds of products for sale. Usually, other salespersons from other suppliers are trying to sell to the same customers that you want to reach. The big questions in sales are: Who gets the order, and why? If you and your competition offer products and services of the same quality and at the same price, why should a customer buy from your business rather than from your competitors?

The answer in most cases is the salesperson. The relationship established between a buyer and a salesperson is a rare combination of business and friendship. Unless you are the only supplier or your prices are far below your competition for the same quality goods, customers have to like you to deal with you. They do not meet you, but they do meet your salesperson. You may be a good businessman or businesswoman and a great person, but that is of little help if your salesperson is unreliable, badly prepared, or objectionable.

A salesperson must have perseverance.

Building friendships and relationships takes time. The fact that a potential customer is not interested in buying one day does not mean that it may not be interested the next. Salespersons must go back to buyers again and again until they soften and buy. Each time the salesperson returns and acts in a friendly and interested manner, showing sincerity and good character, the customer weakens. Eventually, after two, three, or more visits, a sale may be made, and a valuable new account may be opened. Salespersons who give up easily do not belong in the business.

A business should never promise more than it can deliver.

The sales division may have the best salespersons and offer quality products or services in great demand, but it should *never* promise what it cannot deliver. If it promises to deliver on a certain day, it should deliver. If it promises a certain quality for the sales price, it should deliver that quality for that price. If a customer is disappointed or feels it has been misled, the image of the company is tarnished, and this damage cannot easily be repaired. The customer will lose confidence and look elsewhere for supply. If this is to be avoided—and it usually can—the sales force must be in constant communication with the production and accounting divisions.

The sales division must work with the marketing division to promote the sales of the products and services of your business to its customers and have your customers promote your products and services rather than those of your competitors.

A customer may sell and buy the same or similar products and services from three different suppliers. Stores, for instance, may sell 20 different kinds of paper towels, soap, radios, television sets, or processed foods. They make profit on all those products and services and may not care which they sell. It is the job of the sales and marketing divisions to encourage customers to sell your products and services rather than those of your competitors.

To encourage customers to push the sale of one product over another, businesses may offer them promotional discounts if the customer agrees to display its goods in the best-selling area on the premises. A large part of consumer buying is *impulse buying:* Customers often simply notice a product or service before they notice others and, if they feel a need for it, may buy that particular product or service without examining similar goods. If your products or services are displayed where they attract the most notice, your business can benefit most from impulse buying.

For promotional discounts, and sometimes because of the attractiveness of particular advertising posters or materials, customers may allow one supplier to post advertising material on its premises. Again, the name of your product is most obvious, and again, impulse sales will work in your favor.

Sometimes customers do their own advertising, and for a contribution to the cost of that advertising, they will push your products or services in their ads or catalogs. Again, this contributes to the sale of your products and services by calling them to the attention of the customers of your customers.

Sometimes, your business, in cooperation with its customers, can seek to make its products or services more attractive to buyers by reducing prices for a short period of time or providing special prices if a buyer purchases more than one of your products. Often this technique is done using coupons with which the buyer gets a discount. Your customer gets a refund for the discount it allowed when it sends you the coupons it collected for purchases.

Many techniques can be used to promote sales. The most effective, however, is to establish a good relationship with your customers and build confidence in your products or services.

If you use wholesalers, distributors, and agents to help you reach markets, remember that they become your salespersons and therefore should meet your standards.

Wholesalers, distributors, and agents representing you and your

Do your distributors, wholesalers, and agents give the right image of your business?

products and services to product markets can advance or damage your image. They are the ones the customers meet, although they only represent your business. Choose your distributors, agents, and wholesalers carefully and make sure that they are the kind of people you want to represent your business.

Salespersons should never try to cover too much ground.

To do their job properly, salespersons have to spend time with each customer. There must be time allowed for talking shop, developing friendships, and promoting the products and services of the business. If salespersons are assigned too many customers, they cannot devote enough time to each of them, and after a while, customers will feel neglected or underserved. This is often true in retail stores.

By the same token, a salesperson should not cover too large a territory, because too much time spent traveling takes away from the time that is needed for selling and contacting customers.

Therefore, in sales planning, salespersons should be assigned territories and product markets within those territories that they can service to the customers' full satisfaction.

In a certain geographical area—a region, city, district, or county—there may be 15,000 grocery stores or only one steel mill. Every business must establish territories that cover specific product markets; those are the business areas of the operation. Each salesperson must then be given an adequate load of actual or potential customers to keep them busy during the work week.

If there are enough product markets in a given geographical area within your researched business areas, it may take one, two, or more salespersons to properly service them. In any case, sales territories should be planned so as to enable all salespersons to reach their assigned customers with the least possible travel and loss of time.

If customers in product markets are spread out over a large business area, then the customer load must be reduced to allow for travel time between customers. The time lost due to travel must be considered in planning and in determining the costs of the sales division. The primary items of concern in planning and budgeting for the sales division are the number of customers a salesperson can see in a week and the total sales he or she can make in that time.

Remember, time is money in selling too. A business must figure travel time and costs and estimate how many salespersons it will take to sell enough to meet the individual and total sales goals.

The responsibility for checking the credit worthiness of customers belongs to the accounting/finance division.

No products or services should be promised or delivered unless paid for in cash before delivery or cleared as credit worthy by the accounting/finance division. It is the job of the sales division to sell the products and services of the business, not to check credit or decide whether or not customers are financially responsible. Although salespersons may ask new customers for references, they do not check them; the accounting/finance division does.

In small businesses with only a few employees, a single person may technically perform the functions of both accounting/finance manager and sales manager. Nonetheless, both functions exist, and their responsibilities must be kept separate if the business is to succeed.

As your business grows, you can take on fewer functions and concentrate on top management by assigning responsibilities to new employees.

5

Accounting and Finance

After management has researched its markets, conducted marketing studies, developed production goals and set production into motion, and sold its products and services, it must know if it is operating profitably; what its financial condition is; whether the costs budgeted for various divisions are sufficient to let them reach their goals; and whether the money allocated to each division is being used properly. Management must know to which product markets it is selling most and whether its purchasing and production functions are working closely with its marketing and sales functions. It must know if, by what means, and how fast it can expand and where the financial resources for expansion will come from.

Management must watch the unit costs of production and the overall unit costs that reflect the costs of the entire operation. It must keep track of its sales so that it can modify its costs to maintain a sound business balance. Management must know if it must borrow to seize opportunities, how much it can and should borrow, and the best way to obtain the money required to meet its business needs.

All the questions implied by these tasks can be answered by studying the financial statements of a business—the balance sheet and the profit and loss statement. Those statements, prepared by an accountant from the daily journals and ledgers of the organization, are the hard facts about your business and about your management. Businesspeople can fool themselves, and managers may fool themselves, but the hard records of the financial condition of a business can fool no one.

Your financial statements are roadmaps that tell management where it is, where it can go, and the best way to get there.

The financial statements of a business are the road maps that management uses to steer sound courses and directions for the business operation. They tell management where the business is now, where it can go, how fast it can go, and what is the best way to get there.

In plain and straight talk, those managers who do not study their road maps can get lost, and of those who get lost, a great many lose their businesses. Perhaps the greatest cause of business failure is poor financial management.

Yet, financial management does not require a degree in accounting. You can contract with a certified public accountant to service the financial function in your business. To perform a professional service for your business, the accountant can and must prepare financial statements on a regular basis.

The sad fact about many businesses is that management does not appreciate the importance of its financial statements, is unable to use or read them, and does not know how to discuss its financial condition with its accountant. Often, management does not even understand the importance of maintaining proper accounting records.

Businesspeople tend to shy away from areas—such as finance or accounting—in which they have little training or experience. Consequently, they fail to control such functions properly.

If a salesperson, or production worker did not perform well, management would be quick to fire that employee and look for a better person. Management closely watches the performance of its workers, yet it often neglects to measure the performance of its professionals—lawyers, consultants, engineers, architects, and accountants. However, if those people do not perform well for the business, they too should be replaced by more competent professionals.

Often, professionals perform well, but management does not know how to talk to them or what to ask of them. An accountant may do a splendid job of maintaining your records and books but may not reveal "road blocks" or dangers that show up in financial statements. In most cases, management does not ask for this kind of analysis, and some busy accountants may feel that they are not being paid for such service or advice.

Management and its accountant must come to terms and clearly establish what is expected from the accounting function and what responsibilities each has to the other.

The fees charged by an accountant are fair only if management receives the full service it needs to operate its business soundly. If management seeks to save money by paying an accountant less for less service, it may be losing the prime value of the accounting function. Accountants do not merely keep your books and fill out your tax forms; they are specialists qualified to provide management with data and information that are critical to operating the business profitably.

Management must make it clear to its accountant what data it needs, and in cooperation with the accountant, it must work out the time and the costs necessary to insure that the required information is provided.

Your accountant must perform two functions for your business: (1) provide accounting services that detail your operation and its condition at certain periods, and (2) act as a financial adviser and analyze the condition and position of the business at given periods. In the first function, the accountant must report the facts as they are; in the second, he or she must tell you what they mean in terms of your business operation, potentials, business balance, and success and profitability.

If your accountant does not perform those two functions, it means two things: You are not a good manager, and you had better talk to your accountant. Your accounting function calls for both accurate reporting and specific analysis.

To get the full benefit of the accountant's services, management must first understand what the accounting function is all about.

An accounting system is a total process in which all business activities that generate revenues (bring in money) and incur costs (cost money) are recorded. These are summarized at given points in time to let management know where the business stands. That information is also needed to determine what taxes and other charges are due at fixed points in time.

The objective of any accounting system is to maintain records of all of the transactions of a business, and to maintain them properly and accurately so that management can protect the assets of the business—its cash, the money owed it, and so on. Those records must be prepared on a timely basis to meet the needs of the business and the standards and rules established by government or by recognized accounting organizations. Such records include journals and ledgers (records of transactions), which are used to prepare the Income Statement of the business (the statement of profit or loss) and the Statement of Financial Position (the statement describing the assets, the liabilities, and the net worth of the business). These statements will cover a defined period of time (from one identified date to another).

To have its accounting services performed properly and accurately, management must select its accountant carefully.

A manager would not go to a doctor who was not properly trained or engage a lawyer who had insufficient legal training. Yet many managers engage accountants who do not have the training necessary to perform both the accounting and financial analysis functions—or, in some cases, either one of them.

Many businesspeople and managers confuse an accountant with a bookkeeper. The bookkeeper should follow the directions of an accountant and record transactions in journals and ledgers as they happen, day by day. The accountant then takes that information from the records by category and prepares your financial statements, computes your taxes, and summarizes your business condition for management purposes.

An accountant is a professional and should have the necessary training and experience to accurately service your recordkeeping needs, to prepare financial statements according to established government and accounting rules and regulations, and to understand how the financial data bear on your business operation.

Your creditors, your bank, and in some cases your customers decide whether or not they want to do business with you (sell you products or services on credit, lend you money, or buy from you) on the basis of the financial statements of your business.

The financial statements of your business describe the condition of your business, its profitability, and the business outlook. If that picture is bad, you cannot expect banks to lend you money, dealers to give you trade credit, or some large users of your products to feel confident that you can afford to supply their needs.

If your accountant does not prepare your statements properly, maintain your records accurately, or have information available on a timely basis, your image in your markets may be damaged and your business may suffer. You cannot afford that risk.

In choosing an accountant, management must look for many things: proper training, experience, licenses, and references.

In selecting an individual accountant, management should know (1) the individual's education and training (the college or university attended, specialized courses, and any special area of expertise, such as taxation); (2) any licenses, registration, or certification held by the individual (Certified Public Accountant or, for Internal Revenue Service, Public or Registered Accountant); (3) business experience or employment; (4) size of similar accounts; and (5) references that can be checked. Keep in mind that in some instances, only financial statements prepared by a Certified Public Accountant will be acceptable.

In dealing with accounting firms, management should know (1) the size of the firm; (2) the particular person or persons who will be responsible for the account; (3) the number of years the firm has been in business and any special expertise and/or services; and (4) the qualifications of the individual assigned by the accounting firm to service the account.

An accountant, in other words, must be engaged in the same way that you would engage a manager for one of your divisions. You must take the same care and be able to have the same confidence in the person that you would have in one of your managers.

The accountant should be interested in soliciting your views on the weaknesses and strengths of your current system, the needs and desires of your business, and the long- as well as short-range goals of your business. On the other hand, the accountant should not go merely by your word but look over your current system to arrive at an independent evaluation.

The accountant's evaluation, while taking into account the needs, goals, and objectives of the business, should note (1) where deficiencies exist; (2) what controls, checks, and balances are needed; (3) whether the current accounting staff is competent; and (4) what additional staff may be required. In some businesses, a single person, or even top management itself, may be able to act as accounting staff (bookkeeper) with proper instruction and training; in other cases, however, more personnel may be needed.

The accountant should present you with a plan specifying (1) what work is needed; (2) what work will be performed; (3) the time it will take; and (4) what it will cost. Any additional data that will assist the accountant in understanding the business should also be made available.

Once management has determined that the accountant or accounting firm meets its criteria and that the costs are within the financial resources of the business, a "letter of engagement" should be prepared specifying the details of the accountant's responsibilities.

It is management's responsibility to see to it that the contracted accountant or accounting firm is doing its job as agreed upon. It should keep in constant contact with its accountant or firm through oral and/or written communication so as to monitor progress, problems, and new developments.

The most basic aspect of the accounting function that needs constant monitoring is bookkeeping. This is the act of recording the transactions that a business makes in its factor and product markets. It involves the "posting," or recording, of the amounts of individual purchases, sales, and expenses in the company's books (journals) and

Management must see to it that its accountant performs the services for which he or she was contracted.

summary books (ledgers) and the maintenance of all documents that show these purchases, sales, and expenses.

Many small businesses use the single-entry method of bookkeeping.

The single-entry method is based on recording a transaction (buying or selling) in one entry, either in a "sales record book" or an "expense record book." The kind of expense or sale may be described briefly next to the amount—but only in one entry in one book or the other.

Thus, if a company purchased an item for $9.00 for inventory and resale, it would note that purchase in its "expense record book" as

Purchase: item (by name) $9.00

If it sold that item for $10.00, it would note that transaction in one entry made in its "sales record book" as

Sales: item (by name) $10.00

Frequently businesspeople become careless and record wrong amounts or altogether leave out the purchase or the sale.

If an error were made and an entry for a $10.00 sale, for instance, were entered as a $1.00 sale, that mistake would be difficult to notice or correct. Consequently, when all the sales and purchases for a given period of time are added up, they often do not tell management the real amount of money earned as profit or left in the business. Also, to break down items bought or sold into categories and to relate them to factor or product markets becomes a difficult task when records are in such a poor state.

To overcome the problems inherent in the single-entry method, many businesses use the double-entry method of bookkeeping. This method can be a useful tool for analyzing costs and incomes and for planning because it makes it easier to identify the costs of different divisions and the sales to different product markets. However, to derive any benefit from it, management must understand the flow and purpose of accounting transactions and know what books are used at different stages of the accounting process.

In the double-entry method, each transaction is noted under two different *accounts* in one of several *journals*. One of these entries represents a "debit," the other a "credit," and they must *check and balance*; that is, the "debit" must equal the "credit." In this way, it is easier not only to detect mistakes but also to tell what you bought or sold, from whom you bought or to whom you sold, and how much you paid or received. Also, there is less confusion about the amounts of money with which you started out and ended up.

After transactions are recorded, or, in bookkeeping language, "posted," the entries in your different journals represent detailed records that are then ready for further accounting procedures—posting to the *general ledger,* trial balances, and so on.

There are several different journals that must be maintained by your bookkeeper. The most common ones are the *Cash Receipts Journal,* the *Cash Disbursements Journal,* the *Sales Journal,* and the *Purchases Journal.* The Cash Receipts Journal is used *only* when *cash* is received; the Cash Disbursements Journal *only* if *cash* is paid out. If a sale is made against credit, it is recorded in the Sales Journal rather than in the Cash Receipts Journal. Similarly, if a purchase is made on credit, this is entered in the Purchases Journal, not in the Cash Disbursements Journal.

Each of these journals is broken down into several different *accounts.* Some of the most common ones are *Accounts Receivable* (money owed the business by trade customers), *Accounts Payable* (money the business owes to suppliers), *Sales,* and *Inventory.*

The different accounts in the journals (or "books of original entry") will clearly show what transactions have taken place, and the dollar amounts of each transaction will be recorded by the book-keeper on the basis of the documents (bills, sales slips, and so on) used in the transaction.

Some examples will make clear how this works. Suppose a business purchased an item for $9.00 in cash in its factor markets for inventory and resale. It would note that purchase in two entries in its *Cash Disbursements Journal,* namely (1) as a debit under the *Inventory Account* and (2) as a *credit* under the *Cash Account:*

Inventory Account:	(item, supplier)	$9.00 (debit)
Cash Account:	(item, supplier)	$9.00 (credit)

Later, when all debits and credits are totaled up, the two entries in the *Cash Disbursements Journal* would check and balance; if a mistake had been made, this would easily be discovered at that point.

On the other hand, suppose the same purchase had been made on credit. The business would then record this transaction in two entries in the *Purchases Journal:*

Inventory Account:	(item, supplier)	$9.00 (debit)
Accounts Payable:	(item, supplier)	$9.00 (credit)

In both cases, it can tell from the entries that it bought something for $9.00, the purpose for which it was purchased, and how it was bought—for cash or on credit.

In like manner, if the business sold an item for $10.00 in cash, it would enter the sale as a *credit* under the *Sales Account* in the *Cash*

Receipts Journal and as a *debit* under the *Cash Account* in the same journal:

> *Sales Account*: (item, customer $10.00 (credit)
> *Cash Account*: (item, customer) $10.00 (debit)

Again, the two entries, when totaled up, will check and balance, or, if any mistake had been made, it would be detected.

If the same sale had been made against credit, the business would record the transaction in its *Sales Journal* rather than in the *Cash Receipts Journal*:

> *Sales Account:*   (item, customer) $10.00 (credit)
> *Accounts Receivable:*   (item, customer) $10.00 (debit)

The first entry tells the bookkeeper and management that a product was sold for $10.00, and the second, that a credit of $10.00 was extended to a customer. Again, debit and credit balance, or if they do not, the mistake is easily identified and corrected.

Transactions are never considered cash transactions unless cash, checks, or money orders have actually been passed. Once accounts payable and accounts receivable are paid in cash, they become cash transactions. This helps the business know what it has actually paid out or received in cash and how much it owes or is owed in credit.

At the end of a period, usually a month, the bookkeeper will total up all the debits and credits of each account in each journal and enter these total credits and total debits under corresponding accounts in the *general ledger*. Every account that appears in the journals must also appear in the general ledger. From the general ledger, debit and credit balances (net credits or debits) will be used to prepare a "trial balance."

The trial balance is a method of checking that all debit and credit entries are accurate as to their amounts. When the debits do not equal the credits, this indicates that an error has been made, and in this case the bookkeeper or the accountant should analyze the accounts to identify and correct the error. This is important because the financial statements are prepared from the figures in the trial balance.

In our example the general ledger and the trial balance for the two transactions would look as follows:

General Ledger Accounts	Trial Balance Debits	Credits
Sales		$10.00
Purchases (inventory)	$ 9.00	
Cash	1.00	
	$10.00 =	$10.00

The $1.00 cash balance in this case represents profit on sales.

The general ledger and the journals that we have discussed here are not the only books used by businesses. As operations and transactions get more complex, there is a need for other journals, records, or books to ensure control. They may include a *Daily Cash Register* or *Subsidiary Ledgers,* which control certain kinds of transactions under different circumstances. These will not be discussed in depth.

In summary, the flow of bookkeeping and accounting procedures from the moment of a purchase or a sale would look as in Figure 7. The *General Journal* shown in the figure is used for adjustments and error corrections, usually made at the end of the accounting period.

A business may record its transactions either on a "cash basis of accounting" or on the "accrual basis of accounting." When the accounting system is set up on a cash basis, financial transactions are reported as cash is actually received or paid. Under the accrual

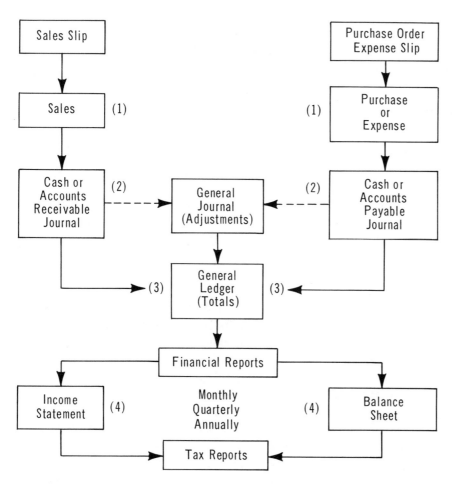

Figure 7. Sequence of bookkeeping and accounting procedures.

system, on the other hand, transactions are reported as income is earned or expenses are incurred, whether or not cash was actually transferred. Each method has its advantage for different businesses. Ask your accountant which is best for you.

When a business sets up its accounting system on a cash basis, it only makes entries when it actually pays for a purchase with cash or actually receives cash for what it sells. If it buys something on Tuesday but does not pay for it until Thursday, it does not make an entry on Tuesday but only on Thursday. If it sells something on Monday but is not actually paid until Friday, it makes no entry on Monday but only on Friday, when it receives the cash from its customer.

Let us say that the business sold something on Monday for $150 and received cash payment. It would then make an entry in its books for that sale. If it bought something on the same day for $100 but did not pay for it immediately, it would make no entry for that purchase on Monday.

Therefore, according to the books, sales were $150 more than purchases since the $100 purchase would not show in the books until actually paid. The business, in other words, would seem to show a profit of $150 although it really owed $100. If purchases had been entered, it would have shown only a $50 profit above the cost of purchases.

In bookkeeping form, the sale would look like this:

Sales:	$150	(credit)
Cash:	$150	(debit)
	-0-	

When the business pays for what it bought, the books would show:

Cash:	$100	(credit)
Purchases:	$100	(debit)
	-0-	

The first double entry shows the money coming into the business, the second, the money going out of the business. This system provides a full picture of all transactions only after they have been paid. Therefore, at a given time, books that are managed on the cash basis may not tell all the facts.

If management opts for the *accrual* basis of accounting, on the other hand, it will record financial transactions as incomes are earned and expenses are incurred. Income earned includes all money owed the business for goods or services sold, whether or not it has actually been paid for them. Expenses incurred are all purchases by the company (materials, supplies, labor, and so on) even if the company has not paid for them. In other words, under this system, all sales and expenses are counted as they happen and not as they are paid. Cash transactions would be handled as they would be in the cash-based system.

Suppose your company sold and delivered $100 worth of goods to a customer on Monday, but the customer did not pay you immediately. If your company operates on the accrual basis of accounting, your bookkeeper will enter the sale in the *Sales Journal,* indicating that payment has not been made but is due as accounts receivable:

Sales Account:	$100.00	(credit)
Accounts Receivable:	$100.00	(debit)
	-0-	

The debit does not say *Cash* but rather *Accounts Receivable.* That means the sale was made, but money was not yet received.

Now, in making the $100 sale, your business reduced its inventory. It must note this in its books too. Let us say that it paid $90 for the goods it sold. In that case, it would set up the following double entry in its general journal:

Cost of Goods Sold:	$90	(debit)
Inventory:	$90	(credit)

When you receive payment for your goods from your customer on Friday, you enter the payment in your cash receipts journal:

Cash Account:	$100	(debit)
Accounts Receivable:	$100	(credit)

As our example illustrates, using accrual basis of accounting enables the business to follow its transactions, whether cash was exchanged or sales or purchases were made on credit. It takes each situation, one at a time, and tells what happened. In the first double entry it showed that a sale was made but not paid for in cash. In the second set of entries it showed that $90 worth of goods was sold from inventory. Finally, in the third double entry it showed that the purchases were paid for by the customer at the sales price (costs and profits) in cash. In the same way, it can tell which purchases were made for cash and which on credit.

The choice of the system your business uses—the cash basis of accounting or the accrual basis of accounting—is significant and may have an impact on the taxes you pay at a given point of time.

For instance, for our two examples the *Income Statement* prepared by the two companies might be as follows:

	Example Used in Cash Basis of Accounting	Example Used in Accrual Basis of Accounting
Sales	$150	$100
Cost of Goods Sold	—	90
Gross Profit	$150	$ 10

The business operating on the cash basis would show an inflated profit since its costs do not show until it pays its bills. The business on the right, which operates on the accrual basis, shows its true profit.

The business operating on the cash basis of accounting would actually have $150 in cash paid to it for the goods it sold. If taxes had to be paid on profits shown, it would pay taxes on $150, even though its actual profit is $50. On the other hand, if it had used the accrual basis instead, its books would have reflected the $100 purchase for which it did not yet pay, and it would have shown a profit of $50 rather than $150.

If the business operating on a cash basis paid the $100 it owed plus the taxes, say $75, on its $150 sale, its costs would add up to $175, or more than it collected for the sales of the goods in the first place. Of course, it might have opted to pay immediately for its $100 purchase and delay collection of $150 in sales until after preparation of its Income Statement. It would then show no profit and pay no taxes.

The second business in our example, namely the one operating on the accrual basis, would not have the money in cash that it needs to pay even its taxes since it had not collected the money for the goods it sold. However, since it operates on credit, it could presumably buy goods without paying for them immediately and pay its taxes and bills for purchases with the money earned from the resale of those goods. Each method, then, has its advantages, depending on how your business operates.

Whether you opt for the cash basis or the accrual basis, your decision should be based on the needs of your business, its objectives, its purchasing and sales practices and policies, and ultimate tax or business advantages. The choice should be worked out between management and its accountant, and it must reflect sound accounting principles and practices and conform to regulations and codes established by the Financial Accounting Standards Board (AICPA), the Internal Revenue Code, the Securities and Exchange Commission (if the business is a public corporation), and other relevant agencies of government.

In addition to preparing reports to management about operations, costs, trends, and the general condition of the business, the accountant is responsible for the preparation of tax returns to federal, state, and local governments.

In preparing tax returns, the accountant follows the instructions and guidelines established by the various tax authorities, which decide which items and moneys are taxable and which can be allowed as deductions. Even though the profit and loss statement of your business may show something entered as a cost or a loss, you may not be allowed to declare it as a cost or a loss under the tax rules set by tax agencies. On the other hand, some items or income that may show as profit or gain may be considered nontaxable or deductible under tax laws.

Therefore, your accountant may prepare a profit and loss statement showing certain costs, incomes, profits, or losses, but in preparing the tax returns of your business the accountant may treat those same items in different ways.

The accountant may be able to save you a large amount of tax payments by applying tax laws to the items in your profit and loss statement. He or she will claim all allowable deductions and exclusions to reduce your taxable profits or increase tax-deductible losses.

Taking advantage of every possible tax benefit is not illegal.

The government agencies that set laws and reporting regulations expect each business to use every legal opportunity to reduce its tax obligations. The laws were made to cover many different kinds of situations. Some businesses may benefit more than others, depending on the circumstances and the rules that are in effect.

Your accountant should not only know sound accounting principles and practices but also be trained and qualified to interpret tax laws and rules for the benefit of the business.

A good accountant may take excellent care of your records and still do a bad service for your business by not maximizing the opportunities to legally reduce business-taxable profits through the use of allowances and exclusions.

You may pay an accountant $1,000, $5,000, or more a year. However, if that person uses his or her knowledge and experience to maximize legal opportunities for reducing your taxable income, your business may save much more than the fees it must pay. That is why it is important to consider the training and experience of an accountant and not just the fees charged.

For example, the Congress of the United States votes on and approves the passage of tax laws. Those laws specifically tell your accountant what deductions (reduction of taxable money) are or are not allowed and what items are excluded from taxation. The accountant only follows the law. If the laws work in your favor, you may be able to reduce your taxable income on the business; if they work against you, your business may have to pay more taxes.

In some cases, your accountant can help management set up operations or transactions so that they legally fall under more favorable tax rules.

Sometimes it is possible to legally make modifications in operations, the structure of the business, or the manner of conducting transactions, which can result in lower taxable income for your business. Your accountant can help you to review your operations and business practices to identify such opportunities.

There may be certain differences between your profit and loss statement and your tax return. These may be either *timing differences* or *permanent differences*. By taking advantage of these differences, you may be able to either postpone payment of a portion of your taxes or permanently save some taxes.

Timing differences between the profit and loss statement and your tax return will eventually be reflected in future financial statements or tax statements. Therefore, they do not reduce the taxes to be paid as much as they allow you to pay them at a later time.

For instance, in accounting there is an item called "depreciation," which applies to capital assets (buildings, machinery, equipment, vehicles, and so on). These assets may be bought at a certain price, but because they do not wear out immediately, the business does not charge the cost as an expense in just one period. Instead, the cost of the asset appears on the balance sheet as a fixed asset (see the discussion later in this chapter).

Because the asset wears out or is used up over many years, the business deducts a certain percentage of the cost over each year. This is perfectly legal; the tax law allows the business this deduction each year over the asset's lifetime of usefulness.

For instance, if a machine were bought for $10,000 and were expected to last ten years, the depreciation expense (allowable deduction) each year could be one-tenth, or $1,000 of the cost of the asset. This is called *straight-line depreciation*. At the end of ten years, the business would be allowed no depreciation for the machine. If it bought a new machine, the depreciation cycle would of course start again. However, under the law, a business may choose to claim a larger depreciation expense for certain assets in the first few years to reduce its taxable income. In later years, the depreciation deduction would then be proportionately smaller. This is called an *accelerated depreciation* method.

If the business expected to show a fair profit at the end of its business year, it might use the accelerated depreciation method to reduce its taxable income. In this way it could depreciate $2,000 each year instead of $1,000, which in accounting is known as double-declining depreciation. In later years, the depreciation for the machine will be used up and therefore no longer be available as a tax deduction. At that point, in other words, the business will have a higher taxable income.

Suppose the business had an income of $5,000 in the first year. Then the two depreciation methods would work as follows:

	Method I (Straight-line)	Method II (Accelerated)
Income	$5,000	$5,000
Depreciation	$1,000 (10 years)	$2,000 (5 years)
Net Income	$4,000	$3,000
Tax (50%)	$2,000	$1,500
Net Profit	$2,000	$1,500

In Method I, the business paid $2,000 in taxes, whereas in Method II, it paid $1,500. This means that Method II left $500 more in the business after taxes even though the statement shows a larger net profit in Method I.

However, in the sixth year, things turn around because the depreciation has been used up in Method II:

	Method I (Straight-line)	Method II (Accelerated)
Income	$5,000	$5,000
Depreciation	$1,000 (10 years)	— (used up)
Net Income	$4,000	$5,000
Tax (50%)	$2,000	$2,500
Net Profit	$2,000	$2,500

Now, Method I ends up with $2,000 in taxes and Method II with $2,500. In other words, the business using the accelerated depreciation method is now paying the taxes it postponed in earlier years.

A *permanent difference* between your profit and loss statement and your tax return occurs when an item is an expense of the company but the Internal Revenue Service does not ever allow a tax deduction for it, or when the business has income that the Internal Revenue Service does not recognize and tax.

There are certain business expenses which the tax laws do not recognize as real expenses, even though they belong in your profit and loss statement. Similarly, there are some incomes that should be reported in the profit and loss statement but are not taxable under the law.

For instance, in business, there is an item called "goodwill." When a firm has been in business for a time, has established itself in product and factor markets, and has built a good name, it considers that its reputation has a certain value. If another business wants to buy that firm, it might pay an additional sum of money for that "goodwill." The goodwill money will not be reflected in something that can be seen or felt; nevertheless, it is valuable to the purchasing company. The buyer can benefit from the reputation that the first business built up through the years.

The financial statements of the purchasing company will show that it paid a certain amount of money for goodwill—an asset. Because goodwill is an intangible rather than a physical asset, it is treated like depreciation, except that it is called amortization. Like a fixed asset, goodwill has to be amortized over its life. Of course, the useful life of goodwill is impossible to determine, but it is generally accepted that it can be from four to forty years.

The purchasing company may decide to charge off goodwill over ten years. Assuming that it paid $10,000 for the goodwill, it would charge off $1,000 a year as an expense on the profit and loss statement.

While the business may deduct $1,000 for goodwill expense, the Internal Revenue Code states that goodwill is not a true cost of business and therefore not a tax-deductible expense. Consequently, the profit and loss statement will show an amortization expense for the goodwill, but the tax returns will not show that expense.

In our example, the profit and loss statement and the tax return of the business for a tax year might look as follows:

	Profit & Loss Statement	Tax Return
Income	$5,000	$5,000
Goodwill	1,000 (estimated)	—
Net Income	$4,000	$5,000
Tax (50%)	2,000 (estimated)	2,500 (actual)
Net Profit	$2,000	$2,500

For the profit and loss statement to reflect actual taxable income, the $1,000 goodwill expense would have to be added to net income, raising taxes by another $500.

Another example of a permanent difference is tax-exempt interest. If a business owns government securities that provide tax-exempt interest, its profit and loss statement would show the interest as income, but this item would not appear on the tax returns of the business. This would make it appear as though the company were paying a lower tax rate; however, the lower tax is due merely to the tax-exempt status of the securities.

Permanent differences, as can be seen from these examples, cannot be changed; they work to the advantage of either the business or the taxing agency, lowering or raising the tax, as the case may be.

There are many more kinds of timing and permanent differences that may occur in your situation, and each has its own method of treatment in records and on tax forms. A business must be concerned with such differences since they can affect the cash left in the business after taxes and thus determine the cash flow of the business.

Your accountant can identify the timing and permanent differences that are relevant to you and inform you of any negative or positive effects they may have on your business.

When you engage an accountant, you should review this person's findings and ask questions. You should ask for suggestions and recommendations and demand timely and responsible service. If you are not satisfied with your accountant's work, change accountants.

Financial statements serve many purposes, and they have a direct effect on your business success.

Management is often busy with the day-to-day matters of operation, supervision, record maintenance, purchasing, or researching changes inside and outside the business. It needs a clear and objective picture of its operations from time to time so as not to lose touch with the business. It has to know where the business is, where it can go, and how it can get there. It needs all the facts, organized in such a way that it can see the entire operation at one time and decide what modifications are required in order to ensure stability and profitability. The financial statements put all of the pieces together. Depending on staff and need, they can be prepared as frequently as every month, but never less frequently than once a year.

Financial statements tell management a multitude of important things.

They tell the business owner or management how many of its products and services were sold, what they cost, and whether the business showed a profit or lost money. They tell how much the business owes, how much is owed to it by customers, and how much cash or inventory remains in the business at a given time. They identify the strengths and weaknesses of the business and indicate where problems may exist in operations or may be developing.

Also, the financial statements tell management whether the business improved over the previous period or periods and whether definite trends are indicated. They may pinpoint opportunities for improvement and expansion and show whether or not the business is operating as well as other businesses in the industry, and whether it has a competitive edge or not.

Finally, they tell management whether or not particular divisions of the business are meeting their level of contribution to overall sales and profits. With these and other data, management can make modifications to improve its operations, staff, or purchasing to restore or improve the business balance.

Management or the business owners are not the only ones interested in how the business is doing.

Others outside the business want to know how well your business is doing. They cannot go into your business and watch what happens for a week or a month. They need all the facts in one place. Your financial statements tell them most of what they need to know.

Government, for instance, wants to know if your business is paying its taxes and meeting various legal obligations. Every business has the responsibility of filing accurate and timely income tax returns with the various federal, state, and local tax authorities. The financial statements are the prime source for the information requested on tax return forms. In addition there are many government agencies, such as the departments of Defense or Commerce, that offer contracts to businesses for all kinds of products and services. In order to determine the capabilities of a business to deliver the supplies needed on time and in the quantities desired, those agencies have to check its financial condition, and again, they use your financial statements for that purpose. The Small Business Administration, the source of many direct and guaranteed loans and contracts, also requires statements covering your current year of operation as well as prior years.

Your creditors, too, want to be informed about the condition of your business.

In businesses where credit buying and selling is the practice, many firms seek some evidence of financial security and responsibility before they will extend credit to a business. No business wants to take unnecessary risks. If your statements show a shaky operation, creditors will not want to take a risk. On the other hand, if the statements show a good report of financial stability, credit will normally be offered.

Creditors determine your credit worthiness by examining your financial statements and by checking with credit-rating agencies, your vendors, or your customers before they make a decision. The credit-rating agencies also want to see your financial statements in order to give your business a rating.

Lending institutions want to know in what shape your business is.

If your business seeks to borrow money from a bank or an individual lender, the lender will want to know the condition of your business before making a loan. Lenders want to be sure that your business will be around until the loan is repaid, and that it will have the funds with which to repay the loan and the interest. Your financial statements over a number of years—provided of course they show financial stability—build the confidence needed to convince the lender that your business is a good risk.

Sometimes, interested parties, like banks, dealers, and government agencies, will not accept statements that are not audited. Audited statements are prepared by an independent body and certify that all of the items reflected in the statements are fairly presented and in accordance with ''generally accepted accounting principles.'' This ''clean bill of health'' by the auditor is an integral part of the statements prepared.

Other parties, such as credit-rating institutions, need your financial statements, too.

There are many credit-rating firms that maintain credit reports on active businesses. These firms are kept abreast of the performance of a business and can give accurate and current information about it to other businesses with which it deals now or which are interested in doing business with it.

To evaluate the financial strengths and weaknesses of any one business, the credit-rating firm examines its financial statements, compares them to industry figures for businesses of similar size and type, and determines its condition and its position in the industry.

A business cannot make its financial statements look good unless it is operating soundly.

Financial statements are made, not imagined, from the results of the business operation. They reflect the real facts about your business. If they say nice things about your business, other businesses want to deal with you; if they say bad things about it, other businesses may not want to deal with you.

Perhaps the most important consideration of all is that management itself must understand the financial statements prepared by its accountant.

A business may get little value from a good accountant or accounting firm if management cannot read or understand the financial statements and cannot communicate effectively with the accountant who provides the service. It is not enough to demand accurate and timely reports from your accountant; management must also know how to use the accounting statements for analysis and planning.

The income statement, also called the profit and loss statement, tells you about the operation in terms of sales, costs, and profits over a period of time. It also indicates how well the different functional divisions of the business are performing.

Income statements conform in many ways to the division into functional areas as previously discussed. For instance, in discussing production, costs are assigned to materials, labor, and overhead. This is reflected in the income statement. Similarly, the costs of the administrative function, the accounting/finance function, and the sales function are all represented on the financial statements.

Unit costs for production and for overall operations can be computed from the figures presented in the statements, as can the costs of purchases and sales. Thus, as a summary of operations, the income statement reveals a lot of essential information about operations, purchases, sales, divisional costs, unit costs, and other details.

Income statements may cover a period of one month, three months (quarterly), six months (semiannual), or a year. They are a measure of performance. By comparing the income statement to the goals established in earlier periods it is possible to tell whether the objectives of the business have been achieved, and if not, why not.

As you read the following, look at the example of an Income Statement in Figure 8. In this way you can follow the items as they are discussed. Keep referring to it as you read.

The first item on the income statement is *Sales*. It is not enough to glance at the income statement of your business and be happy because sales were higher than last time. Any entry by itself, including net profit, does not tell the entire story. We have already seen that sometimes statements can show items that are not acceptable on tax returns.

Sales represents total sales (goods sold) before adjustments for discounts or returns. The business owner or management must consider whether a higher or lower sales figure represents actual sale of more or less units or reflects sales price modifications. Obviously, if prices were raised, it would take fewer units to reach the sales figure reported. On the other hand, if prices were lowered, it would take more units sold to reach the sales figure. Just as important, management must not be impressed by sales without first looking at profits. Theoretically, the cost of each unit sold may be higher than its sales price, in which case the business would have operated at a loss.

By comparing current sales figures to those of previous years and

Figure 8. Income Statement, XYZ Manufacturing, Inc., period ending as of December 31, 1976.

Sales:			$105,000
Less: Returns & Allowances			5,000
Net Sales			100,000
Cost of Goods Sold			
Inventory 1/1/76	$10,000		
Purchases	39,000		
Freight In	500		
Cost of Goods Available		$49,500	
Less: Inventory 12/31/76		15,000	
Cost of Goods		34,500	
Wages & Taxes—Factory		21,800	
Depreciation—Factory		1,200	
Depreciation—Equipment		2,500	
Cost of Goods Sold			60,000
Gross Profit			40,000
Operating Expenses			
Selling Expenses			
Commissions	2,000		
Salaries	10,400		
Travel	1,000		
Depreciation—Vehicles	700		
Freight Out	800		
Miscellaneous Selling	100		
Total Selling Expense		15,000	
General & Administrative			
Salaries—Officer	7,000		
Office	3,000		
Interest (Mortgage)	1,800		
Interest (Bank)	2,000		
Utilities	1,200		
Office Expenses	2,400		
Depreciation—Office	1,000		
Professional Fees	1,600		
Total General & Administrative		20,000	
Total Operating Expenses			35,000
Net Income before Taxes			5,000
Taxes (at 22%)			1,100
Net Profit			$ 3,900

relating them to the number of units sold, sales prices, unit costs, and profits, management can evaluate its true sales patterns.

Right under *Sales* on the Income Statement can be found an item, called "Returns and Allowances," which affects the total sales figure. If a business produces products or services of irregular or inferior quality, purchasers may return the products or seek credit for the services. In many cases, customers return products because they change their minds or because the products do not fit or in other ways fail to meet the customers' needs. Also, sometimes, when demand is low, a business will sell its products at special prices or make other allowances to generate sales. The sales figures must be adjusted to reflect the sales price of the products returned by customers and the true cost of the allowances provided as incentives to customers.

Net Sales is the adjusted total sales figure for the period, after returns and allowances have been deducted. If the return and allowance figure is high, management knows that either it has a problem with quality control or its products are not in strong demand. This means that management must take a good look at its marketing and production functions. It can be seen, then, that each line on the Income Statement not only reports facts but also indicates potential trouble spots.

Sometimes deliveries are slow, and shipments are refused by customers as too late for the season. Sometimes discounts may be too low to meet competition. Each possibility must be questioned and studied.

The next item on the Income Statement is *Cost of Goods Sold*. This category relates to the costs of the production division. If you will recall, there are three main categories in production: materials, labor, and overhead. The costs shown on the Income Statement for production relate solely to goods or services actually sold.

Materials (inventory) are covered in three parts: the inventory at the beginning of the accounting period, purchases for inventory during this period, and the inventory that remains at the end of the accounting period covered by the report. Inventory is valued on its historical cost (price for the inventory when purchased) or its market value (price for the inventory if you had to replace or reproduce the same inventory). Whichever is lower—cost or market—is the value attached to the inventory.

Freight In represents the cost of getting the purchases of inventory into the production division. It is included as part of the cost of inventory. It should be noted that the Income Statement in Figure 8 is used for illustrative purposes only; it is not as detailed as one that would be prepared for a manufacturing concern in the real world. In practice, the *Cost of Goods* section, as far as materials is concerned, would be broken down into raw materials on hand and purchased, materials in process, and materials that are completely processed (finished) and in the warehouse.

Labor is covered by the item *Wages and Taxes*, which represents the cost of all the labor in the factory. It must be remembered, however, that the labor costs in a factory are of two types: *direct labor* (employees who work directly on the product) and *overhead* (the costs of the supervisors, managers, and others not directly involved in handling or processing goods).

The other items in the *Cost of Goods Sold* section are part of the overhead of the production division. They include the depreciation on the equipment that is used to produce the product, the depreciation on the factory portion of the building, and all other expenses, although not shown in our statement, that occur in the factory and are not either direct labor or materials costs; utilities, oils for maintenance, and factory supplies would fall under this latter category.

The total under *Cost of Goods Sold* in line 14 shows the true cost of the products or services you delivered, after adjustments for inventory, wages, taxes, depreciation, and other expenses. Goods that were produced but not sold were subtracted from the total of goods available, leaving only those goods produced and sold in the accounting period.

Now that all the items in *Cost of Goods Sold* have been identified, let us examine them for their other meanings to management.

If the starting inventory carried over from the previous period is large, management must ask itself why this is the case. If production was normal during the last period and the products sold at a significantly lower level, then planning may not have been sound. Either too much was produced in the previous period considering demand or available money in product markets, or for some reason customers did not buy your goods, even though demand and buying power were adequate. Perhaps the quality or the design was poor, or the sales prices were too high. Discounts may have been too low. Maybe your sales division did not do its job, or your marketing division did not research properly or came up with the wrong conclusions. Perhaps delivery was poor, or your materials came in too slowly to meet your schedules. Perhaps the drop in sales was due to interruptions (strikes, fires, and so on) in your business or in your product markets. All possibilities must be considered.

If inventory at the beginning is too low, this may mean that you are not producing fast enough, that you cannot get the supplies you need, or that you do not have enough money in the business to pay for the materials you need. If inventory carried over from previous periods is too low, it may spell trouble too.

If at the end of the period covered by the Income Statement there are too many goods unsold (ending inventory), that could mean that your sales prices were too high, that the demand for your products has dropped, that your sales force is sleeping, that your competitors are taking your customers from your business, that the quality of your products has slipped and customers have lost confidence, or that there were interruptions in your or your customers' operations.

Management, as we have seen, must also be concerned with the unit cost of production. This cost should be compared with costs for previous periods. It may show a higher or lower amount. In either case, management should study these costs to determine where the changes stem from—materials, labor, or overhead—and what methods can be used to correct negative trends.

The next item on the Income Statement is *Gross Profit*. This is the difference between *Net Sales* and *Cost of Goods Sold* and represents the margin available to the business to cover its operating expenses, that is, the costs of administration, sales, accounting, and so on. It also provides a rough measure of the profitability and efficiency of the production division.

The next major category in the Income Statement, namely *Operating Expenses,* covers the costs of other divisions, units, or functions.

Selling Expenses refers to the costs of the sales division. They would include salaries for the staff in the division, commissions paid to salespersons (a percentage based on the sales they make), travel expenses for the sales staff, the depreciation costs for cars or trucks used by the salespersons, shipping costs for goods sold and delivered, and miscellaneous costs chargeable to the sales division. *Total Selling Expense* is the sum of all of these costs.

Selling expenses should be compared to those for previous periods. If sales remain more or less constant but selling costs go up, management should know the reasons for that change. If selling costs go down, management should also know why this happened. Perhaps unit sales dropped and sales prices increased. In that case, a smaller sales force would have produced a higher net sales result. On the other hand, if selling expenses were high without a corresponding change in the net sales figure, this may mean that more products or services were sold at lower prices, with more salespersons needed. Maybe shipping costs rose and the business had to increase its sales prices to absorb part of that cost. Maybe the sales division is not performing its function well. Whatever the reasons for changes from period to period, management should know them.

The next category under *Operating Expenses* is *General & Administrative.* This item reflects the cost of the accounting/finance division and of administration and management, including any outside professionals, for instance, accountants or lawyers, who are not on staff as salaried employees.

Salaries—Officer can mean several things. A person can own a business and not work in it. As an officer of the corporation, he or she may draw a regular salary. On the other hand, the business owner may work in the business and draw a salary. Salaries for ownership are regular payments and should not be confused with the net profit of the business. Net profits may be taken out by owners in addition to their salaries, but they are not part of the regular payroll expenses for the administration division.

Businesses that operate as corporations may file a ''Subchapter S'' application with the Internal Revenue Service. In that case, ownership may treat all profits and salaries drawn by it as income, and the business will then pay no income taxes. If a business is not operated as a corporation under Subchapter S, it must first pay income taxes on the profits earned by it, and the owners or stockholders must again pay a personal income tax on any portion of net profits distributed to them. Under Subchapter S, then, all business profits and salaries are treated as ordinary income to the owners or stockholders, and they, not the business, pay the taxes.

Ask your accountant which status is best for you and your business.

Salaries—Office refers to the costs for salaries paid to office personnel—secretaries, clerks, bookkeepers, and other staff of the accounting/finance division.

Interest—Mortgage refers to interest paid on money owed to a lender for the purchase of equipment, land, or buildings. *Interest—Bank* refers to expenses for borrowing money from a bank.

Depreciation—Office refers to the depreciation on the portion of the facilities that is used for administrative purposes; this does not include the factory space. In our example, the building is owned by the firm; if it were not, the caption for this expense would be *Rent*.

Finally, *Professional Fees* are monies paid to outside professionals, as illustrated in our functional organization charts. These individuals may be lawyers, accountants, consultants, and so on, who are not on the firm's payroll as employees.

Total General & Administrative expenses is the sum total of all the costs in this category.

Management must again compare the costs of this category with those for prior years. If the costs of this category rose, management should know the reason for the increase. Maybe additional staff was needed in the bookkeeping area because of increased sales. Maybe the cost of office utilities, labor, or supplies increased. Management must make sure that costs in this category are not too high for the overall operation.

Total Operating Expenses is the sum total of the Selling and General and Administrative costs. They are deducted from the *Gross Profit* to arrive at the *Net Income before Taxes*.

Taxes refers to the taxes owed federal, state, and local government agencies on the firm's income.

Net Profit refers to what is left after all costs and taxes are accounted for. Net profits are the monies available for distribution to owners or for meeting the future needs of the business.

To help management evaluate the operation of the business, your accountant can prepare an *Analysis of Operations* from the Income Statement. Figure 9 shows an example of such a report. A short explanation of the items shown in that example follows.

Column 1. Sales and expenses are taken from the Income Statement for the previous year (1975).

Column 2. For ease of analysis, all amounts in column 1 are converted to percentages. Sales of $90,000 represent 100 percent,

Figure 9. Analysis of Operations (Income Statement), XYZ Manufacturing, Inc.

	Prior Year (1975)		Current Year (1976)				
	$000	Percent	$000	Budget ($000)	(Under) or Over Budget	Company (Percent)	Industry (Percent)
Sales (net)	90	100	100	125	(25)	100	100
Cost of goods	62	68.9	60	75	(15)	60	70
Gross profit	28	31.1	40	50	(10)	40	30
Selling expense (less depreciation)	13	14.4	15	20	(5)		
General & administrative (less depreciation)	18	20	20	22	(2)	35	23
Operating profit	(3)	(3.3)	5	8	(3)	5	7
Other income	.5	.5	—	—	—		
Other expenses	—	—	—	—	—		
Profit before taxes	(2.5)	(2.8)	5	8	(3)	5	7
Tax			1.1	—	—		
Net profit			3.9	—	—		

the other amounts are converted into percentages by dividing each amount by sales and multiplying by 100 percent.

Column 3. These are the figures that are taken from the Income Statement for the current year (1976).

Column 4. These figures are taken from the budget prepared by management at the beginning of the current year.

Column 5. The figures represent the difference between management's budget (column 4) and the actual amounts shown in column 3.

Column 6. The amounts in column 3 are converted to percentages for comparison with average industry performance (column 7).

When management reviews this analysis, it can determine if the company's operation has improved from year to year and how the company compares to the industry to which it belongs.

As we have seen, it does not take an expert to identify many areas of concern in the Income Statement. Although it may not be able to interpret the statement in the same depth as a skilled financial analyst, management can quickly notice many changes that should be investigated. By studying changes from period to period, management can follow trends in its operations and locate areas that can be modified without interrupting operations or causing the business to lose sight of its goals.

The next statement prepared by your accountant is the balance sheet. This statement tells management what it owns (and the value of what it owns), what it owes, and what is owed to the business. It identifies strengths and weaknesses and the resources that are available at a given period to operate the business.

Figure 10. Balance Sheet, XYZ Manufacturing, Inc., period ending as of December 31, 1976.

ASSETS

Current Assets		
Cash		$ 3,000
Accounts Receivable	$ 8,000	
Less: Allowance for Bad Debts	500	7,500
Inventory 12/31/75 (lower of cost or market)		15,000
Prepaid Expenses		500
Total Current Assets		$26,000
Fixed Assets		
Equipment—Factory	25,000	
Less: Accumulated Depreciation	7,500	17,500
Vehicles	3,500	
Less: Accumulated Depreciation	700	2,800
Furniture & Fixtures	5,000	
Less: Accumulated Depreciation	2,000	3,000
Land & Building	38,000	
Less: Accumulated Depreciation	3,600	34,400
Total Fixed Assets		57,700
Total Assets		$83,700

LIABILITIES & STOCKHOLDERS' EQUITY

Current Liabilities		
Notes Payable—Bank (Current Portion)	$ 7,000	
Mortgage Payable (Current Portion)	1,800	
Taxes Payable	2,000	
Accounts Payable	3,900	
Total Current Liabilities		$14,700
Long-Term Liabilities		
Mortgage Payable	32,600	
Notes Payable—Bank	7,000	
Total Long-Term Liabilities		39,600
Total Liabilities		$54,300

Stockholders' Equity

Capital Stock—1,000 shares common stock		
authorized and issued, $5.00 par value	5,000	
Paid-in Capital in excess of par value	20,000	
Total Paid-in Capital		25,000
Retained Earnings—12/31/74	500	
Retained Earnings—12/31/75	3,900	4,400
Total Stockholders' Equity		29,400
Total Liabilities & Stockholders' Equity		$83,700

The Balance Sheet is a statement of financial position. It is comprised of three sections. The first section covers *assets,* the second *liabilities,* and the third *capital* or *stockholders' equity.* These are broken down into subcategories that give further information about each category.

    Figure 10 gives an example of a Balance Sheet. As we discuss the items contained in it, please refer to the figure; this will make it easier to follow the points that will be raised.

Assets are those things in a business which the business owns or in which it has an interest. These cover two types of assets: (1) *current assets* represent things that can be used or converted into cash within the operating cycle of the business, usually one year; (2) *fixed assets* are those things that will not be used up or converted into cash within the normal operating cycle of the business.

While the company owns assets, it may owe money for them. For instance, a business may buy a truck but pay only one-third down and owe the rest in mortgage payments. The Balance Sheet will list the truck and its cost as a fixed asset and the mortgage (balance owed) as a liability. In this way, it can be seen immediately that the business has an interest in the truck (it owns it although it has not fully paid for it) but still owes money on the truck mortgage. This works in the same way for all items purchased in this manner.

The first item under *Current Assets* is *Cash*. This is cash on hand (in the business) or in the bank, or both. Under *Marketable Securities*, we would include all stocks and bonds that have a ready market (are easily bought and sold); an example would be government securities. These types of securities are said to be "liquid" because of the ease with which they can be converted into cash.

The next item under *Current Assets, Accounts Receivable,* refers to the money owed to the business by its customers for products or services sold but not paid for at the time the Balance Sheet was prepared. Although the money under this item is shown as a current asset and is assumed to be convertible into cash within the business cycle, some of it may in fact not be paid by the customers. If a business does not check the credit worthiness of its customers before selling to them, it may find that many of them were poor credit risks. The accounts receivable, in other words, are only as good as the customers that owe them.

It is for this reason that an *Allowance for Bad Debts* account is established. If a customer does not pay its bill within a reasonable period of time, the business must assume that it will never be paid. Sometimes a customer may go bankrupt and be unable to pay. In this event, the business cannot continue this account as a good receivable but must deduct this amount from its receivables total. The *Bad Debt* account allows for this possibility.

The next item under *Current Assets* is *Inventory*. Inventory states the value of the goods that have not been sold. To establish a fair value, the business cannot use *its* sales prices as a measure, because prices may change up or down. Therefore, a standard method of valuating is used, namely the lower of cost or market value.

Prepaid Expenses refers to certain expenses that were paid in advance. If your business paid in advance for its rent or for utilities, this would be noted as prepaid expenses in the Balance Sheet. Money paid in advance of the date when it is due is treated as an asset of the

Assets are what the business owns.

company. If for some reason the business needs the money it prepaid, it has a right to that money since it has not received the corresponding goods or services yet.

Total Current Assets is merely the sum total of all the assets in that category.

The first item under *Fixed Assets, Equipment—Factory* notes the value of the machinery, equipment, and tools owned by the business. They are valued at their cost. Because the equipment wears out in time, the business depreciates a certain amount of its cost every year over its useful life. This depreciation is increased each year for as long as the item is kept in service or use. The *Accumulated Depreciation* category represents the total depreciation expense deducted up to the present time for each item. This indicates the book value of the equipment and gives an idea of its remaining usefulness.

All items that the business owns or in which it has an interest must be noted in the *Assets* section.

The next major category on the Balance Sheet is *Liabilities and Stockholders' equity*. Liabilities are the debts and obligations of the business, that is, the money owed by it. Stockholders' equity is what remains after the liabilities (what is owed by the business) are subtracted from the assets (what the business owns or has an interest in).

Liabilities are what the business owes.

Liabilities are of two types: *current* and *long-term*. Current liabilities are debts or obligations that must be repaid within one year from the date of the statement; long-term liabilities are those that are to be repaid at a later time.

Under *Current Liabilities,* the first item is *Notes Payable—Bank (Current Portion).* The second item is *Mortgage Payable (Current Portion).* In both these cases the business borrowed money—in the first case, for working capital, in the second, for purchasing buildings or equipment.

If a business wants to buy land or a building but does not have the total amount of money needed, it might go to a bank and borrow the money. The bank will hold a mortgage on the land or building until the loan is repaid in full, and the business will pay a portion of the mortgage each year. The portion that is due each period by the business appears on the Balance Sheet as a current liability. The balance of the mortgage, which will take several years to pay,back, is considered a long-term liability. The same holds true with a bank loan. The portion due within the business cycle, usually a year, will be treated as a current liability, and the balance will appear as *Notes Payable* under *Long-Term Liabilities.*

The third item, *Taxes Payable,* refers to taxes that are owed to the government and have not yet been paid. This does not mean that the business is in arrears (has not paid its taxes) but rather that business or payroll taxes may have been collected but have not yet been sent to the government because the tax due date has not arrived.

Accounts Payable refers to money owed by the business to its suppliers for materials or services bought on credit.

Total Current Liabilities is the total of all the current liabilities of the business.

The second category of liabilities is *Long-Term Liabilities. Mortgage Payable* in this section represents the portion of mortgage not payable within one year from the date of the statement, which is the usual duration of the business cycle. Similarly, *Notes Payable* represents the portion of bank loans that is payable after more than one year.

Total Long-Term Liabilities is the sum total of all long-term liabilities, and *Total Liabilities* represents all the liabilities of the business, both current and long-term.

In the example shown in Figure 10, it can be seen that the assets of the business exceed its liabilities. Clearly, this is good. If the liabilities were to exceed the assets, it would mean that the business is in trouble, if not bankrupt. In many industries, the condition of a business is measured by comparing its liabilities to its assets. If the business has great assets and comparatively small liabilities, this generally means that it will have little trouble paying its debts. The closer the two amounts get, the more difficult it may be for a business to pay all of its debts. If a bank or a supplier were considering lending you cash or extending credit to you for supplies, it would look at such ratios to determine whether or not you are a good risk.

Lenders and creditors would also look at certain items to figure out how much ready cash the business has available to it. If most of the money were tied up in fixed assets, the business would not be able to convert them to cash in a hurry, if needed. It could, however, sell government securities quickly, or even give discounts to its customers on outstanding bills to encourage quick payment. Also, its inventory might be sold off in a short time if it needed money.

Thus, the more current assets a business has, the better access it may have to ready cash. However, certain items in the current assets are not as easily converted into cash as others, and lenders or creditors will pay some attention to this possibility. For instance, the finished or unfinished goods in your inventory may not be of the type that is currently in demand.

The comparison of current assets to current liabilities is one of many formulas used to analyze the Balance Sheet. There are many others, commonly referred to as business ratios or financial ratios. Examples and explanations for some of the financial ratios can be found later in this section.

The third category on the Balance Sheet is *Stockholders' Equity*. This is the difference between assets and liabilities and represents what is actually left to the owners of the business if all the debts and obligations of the business were paid.

The first item under *Stockholders' Equity* is *Capital Stock*. In a corporation the "owners" of the business are its stockholders. The business files with the state government as a corporation and states in its registration that a certain number of shares are to be authorized. It can then "issue" (sell) all or part of those shares to raise the capital with which to operate the business.

When the corporation issues the stock, it sets a value on each share. This value is called the *par value*. In our example, 1,000 shares were authorized and issued at a par value of $5.00 each. This raised a start-up capital of $5,000 for the corporation. A corporation may also issue stock that has been authorized with no par value. The decision as to how the company stock is to be issued should be made by management in collaboration with qualified lawyers and accountants.

In an unincorporated business, the initial investment of money by the owners would correspond to the initial sale of stock in a corporation. This would simply be called *Owner Capital*.

Paid-in Capital in excess of par value refers to the sale of the same 1,000 shares. In our case, it states that when the 1,000 shares were sold, they commanded $20,000 above their par value. For reasons we will not discuss, the value above par must be stated separately.

Total Paid-in Capital refers to all the money paid for shares sold, at par or above par.

Retained Earnings refers to net profits after taxes that were kept in the business. In a corporation, the net profits after taxes can be distributed among the stockholders as dividends or be kept in the business as working capital. If the business is not a corporation, or if it is a corporation operating under "Subchapter S" status, the profits of the business, as we have seen earlier, become part of the income of the owners and are taxed as such.

Total Stockholders' Equity is the sum total of all money raised through sale of stock and all money earned and retained in the business over its lifetime.

If you will notice, the last item, *Total Liabilities and Stockholders' Equity*, equals the total of all assets. This is always true, hence the name Balance Sheet.

The Balance Sheet tells a lot about your business. It tells how much you really own of your business, how great the assets of the business are, and how much of these assets the business really owns. It tells how much you must pay out to meet your debt and when, and how much is left after those payments. It tells whether you are too heavy in fixed assets and too poor in liquid assets that are easily converted into cash. It tells how much you invested and where additional capital came from (stock sales, earnings, and so on). It tells how much money is owed to the business by customers and others and how much you owe customers, suppliers, and lenders.

If the amount of money owed to suppliers and others is greater than that owed the company by customers, this could be an indication that the company has a tight cash situation or that its operating expenses are too high.

Furthermore, the Balance Sheet tells you how much was borrowed and what it was used for—working capital, acquisition of machinery, equipment, or property, and so on. And it indicates the condition of various fixed assets by stating their accumulated depreciation. From the depreciation amount noted on the Balance Sheet it will be clear immediately whether a given piece of equipment or property is new, is used up partially or almost completely, or needs to be replaced.

Information contained in the Income Statement is reflected in the Balance Sheet. Each kind of statement tells part of the story; together they tell the entire story about a business.

Sales and purchases on the Income Statement show in the Balance Sheet. If they were made for cash, they would show as *Cash* or *Inventory* on the Balance Sheet. If they were bought or sold on credit, they would show as *Accounts Receivable* or *Accounts Payable* on the Balance Sheet. Similarly, any depreciation noted in the Income Statement also shows on the Balance Sheet within the accumulated depreciation category.

Every business owner or manager should examine the Income Statement and Balance Sheet of the business.

Some items will be easily identified, as will some problems; others will require a deeper analysis. In any case, if you spend some time with your accountant reviewing the statements and their meaning, you will learn the things about your operation that are critical to its sound operation and success. Such a review of the accounting statements should be part of the accounting services you contract. Make sure it is included when your business and your accountant set up the contract, or you will lose most of the benefits of a sound accounting service.

Here are definitions and ratios that are commonly used by accountants, banks, credit-rating businesses, creditors, and others. The figures given in this group of formulas are taken directly from the Income Statement (Fig. 8) and Balance Sheet (Fig. 10) for XYZ Manufacturing, Inc.

Balance Sheets and Income Statements are directly related.

Current Assets (CA)	= the amount noted on the Balance Sheet as total *Current Assets* ($26,000)
Current Liabilities (CL)	= the amount noted on the Balance Sheet as total *Current Liabilities* ($14,700)
Current Ratio (CR)	= total *Current Assets* (CA) divided by total *Current Liabilities* (CL): CA ÷ CL = CR
Working Capital (WC)	= total *Current Assets* (CA) minus total *Current Liabilities* (CL): CA − CL = WC
Quick Assets (QA)	= total *Current Assets* (CA) minus *Slow Assets* (SA), that is, items not quickly convertible to cash, such as inventory or prepaid items, etc. CA − SA = QA
Quick Ratio (QR)	= *Quick Assets* (QA) divided by *Current Liabilities* (CL): QA ÷ CL = QR
Average Inventory (AI)	= the *Beginning Inventory* from the Income Statement ($10,000) plus the *Ending Inventory* ($15,000), divided by 2: $$\frac{10{,}000 + 15{,}000}{2} = \$12{,}500$$
Inventory Turnover (IT)	= *Average Inventory* ($12,500) divided by *Cost of Goods Sold* ($60,000), times 360 days: $$\frac{12{,}500}{60{,}000} \times 360 \text{ days} =$$ 0.2083 × 360 days = 75 days
Receivable Turnover	= the *Accounts Receivable* figure after deducting the allowance for bad debts ($8,000 − $500 = $7,500) divided by *Net Sales* ($100,000), multiplied by 360 days: $$\frac{7{,}500}{100{,}000} \times 360 \text{ days} =$$ 0.075 × 360 days = 27 days
Long-Term Debt	= the *Long-Term Liabilities* figure on the Balance Sheet
Net Worth	= the amount noted on the Balance Sheet as *Net Worth, Capital,* or *Stockholders' Equity.*

Figure 11 shows a *Balance Sheet Analysis,* such as might be prepared by your accountant, that is based on these definitions and ratios.

Management, with the advice of its accountant, must select the inventory reporting method that is best suited to the needs of the business and provides the best tax benefits.

Figure 11. Balance Sheet Analysis, XYZ Manufacturing, Inc.

	Last Period 1975	This Period 1976	Comparison Periods 1975 vs 1976	Industry Ratios*
Current Assets	$23,500	$26,000	$2,500	—
Current Liability	10,700	14,700	4,000	—
Working Capital	12,800	11,300	(1,500)	—
Long-Term Debt	34,400	39,600	5,200	—
Net Worth	25,500	29,400	3,900	—
Current Ratio	2.1	1.8	1.3	1.9
Quick Ratio	1.2	.7	.5	.9
Inventory Turnover	58 days	75 days	17 days	36 days
Accounts Receivable Turnover	36 days	27 days	9 days	33 days

*These industry ratios are not based on actual figures nor taken from any of the publications cited. They were devised solely for illustrative purposes. A useful source for actual industry ratios are the *Annual Statement Studies* published by Robert Morris Associates, Philadelphia.

Inventory represents a sizable expenditure of a business. We have seen that inventory shows on both the Income Statement and the Balance Sheet. In the Income Statement it represents part of *Cost of Goods,* and in the Balance Sheet it is part of *Current Assets.* Using as example our business in Figures 10 and 12, these items would appear as follows:

Abstract of Income Statement

Cost of Goods Sold		
Beginning Inventory	$10,000	
Purchases	39,000	
Freight in	500	$49,500
Less: Ending Inventory		15,000
Cost of Goods		$34,500

Abstract of Balance Sheet

Current Assets	
Cash	$ 3,000
Accounts Receivable (net)	7,500
Inventory	15,000
Prepaid Expenses	500
Total Current Assets	$26,000

The accountant must set a value on the inventory. This value is always the lower of *cost* (what was paid), or *market value* (the prices paid to replace or reproduce such goods in today's markets). Also, the method in which the inventory flows through the business, and ultimately to the customer, is a determining factor.

Two of the most common methods of setting a value on inventory are the First-In-First-Out (FIFO) method and the Last-In-First-Out method (LIFO).

In the FIFO method, the first purchases placed in inventory are treated as those that are sold first. Suppose that at the beginning of the business year, you bought 3,000 items for inventory at a *cost* of $1.00 per item, and an additional 2,000 items later in the year for $1.25 per item. Then if at the close of the reporting period for an Income Statement or Balance Sheet 1,000 items were left in your inventory, they would be valued, under the FIFO method, at $1.25 each, rather than $1.00. Therefore, the value of your ending inventory would be set at $1,250.

Under the LIFO method, on the other hand, the last purchases for inventory at a cost of $1.25 are considered sold before the first purchases at $1.00. Therefore, if this method were used, your ending inventory would be valued at $1.00 per item, not $1.25, yielding a total value for your ending inventory of $1,000.

Figure 12(a) and 12(b) summarize this situation. Note that in order to use the FIFO method, you need not actually *sell* the items purchased first before selling inventory items purchased later; you may sell them in any order that is convenient. LIFO and FIFO are merely methods for *valuing* your remaining inventory at the end of the accounting period.

These two methods affect Income Statements and Balance Sheets in different ways. First compare the effects of the FIFO and LIFO methods on Income Statements. Taking the simple case of an inventory of two items only, one purchased first for $1.00, the other later for $1.25, the FIFO method might lead to the following Income Statement:

Income Statement

Sales (one item)		$2.00
Beginning Inventory	—	
Purchases ($1.00 + $1.25)	$2.25	
Less: Ending Inventory (FIFO)	1.25	
Cost of Goods		1.00
Gross Profit		$1.00

For the same situation, the LIFO method (Last-In-First-Out) would result in the following Income Statement:

Income Statement

Sales (one item)		$2.00
Beginning Inventory	—	
Purchases ($1.00 + $1.25)	$2.25	
Less: Ending Inventory (LIFO)	1.00	
Cost of Goods		1.25
Gross Profit		$ .75

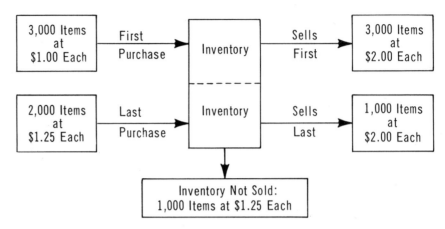

Figure 12(a). Inventory valuation under the FIFO method.

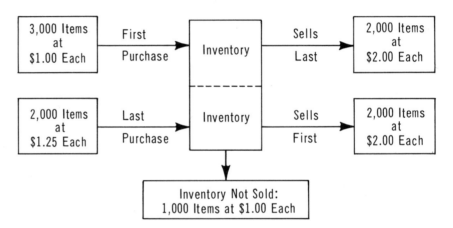

Figure 12(b). Inventory valuation under the LIFO method.

In the FIFO method, the gross profit is $1.00; in the LIFO method, it is $.75. In actual business figures involving many thousands of dollars in inventory purchases, the difference can clearly be considerable. The larger the gross profit, the larger the potentials for net profits (but also the taxes the business must pay).

Consider now the effects of FIFO and LIFO on the Balance Sheet. First let us look at the FIFO method for the example used for the Income Statement:

Balance Sheet

Current Assets	
Cash	$1.00
Other	1.00
Inventory (FIFO)	1.00
Total Current Assets	$3.00

Under the LIFO method, the same situation would be recorded as follows:

Balance Sheet

Current Assets		
Cash		$1.00
Other		1.00
Inventory (LIFO)		1.25
Total Current Assets		$3.25

In the FIFO method, the total current assets were $3.00, whereas in the LIFO method, they were $3.25. Again, the significance would become apparent if real inventory figures were used.

Depending on the kind of business, the choice of the LIFO or FIFO method is important. In an industry where the costs of raw materials, for instance, metals or chemicals, vary to greater degrees, the impact of the choice on the financial statements can be considerable.

There are other methods of valuation as well. Your business must choose the one best for it. The selection must be made by management with the help of the accountant. The determining factors are the needs and objectives of your business, but economic considerations, rising or falling costs for materials, and government regulations and tax laws also play a part.

The responsibility for choosing an inventory valuation method must be assigned to both management and its accountant. That choice must be made after the impact of different methods on the financial statements, prices, and taxes has been carefully studied.

In summary, financial management of a business is just as important as buying and selling or production. Your accountant must assist management in this through advice, explanations, and regular reviews of the accounting statements with management.

6

What It All Means

Business is in many respects like a jungle where everybody must fight for survival.

In a free enterprise system, there exists opportunity for all to enter into business and to succeed, provided they are willing to work hard. Because anyone can start a business, many do, and the competition for markets, supply, labor, and capital becomes greater as more and more people go into business.

In most cases, the business you choose is also chosen by hundreds or thousands of other people. In each industry, industrial group, or business category there are a great many businesses competing with each other.

As shown in the previous materials, all industries and businesses, in many ways, also compete with one another.

The business whose management is best prepared has the greatest chance of surviving and prospering.

There are only so many customers for certain products and services, and they have only so much money to spend on them. The business with the most informed and alert management is in the best position to capture sales and markets and earn profits. Since most businesses are small and have limited resources, they cannot afford substantial losses or risks. That is why one out of every two new businesses fail in the United States each year.

The difference could easily be the competence of business management. Management must not only know how to operate its business and use outside professionals, but also understand what inside and outside factors affect the business and how to identify and evaluate them.

With knowledge and information, management can keep modifying its operations to meet changes. It can reduce the impact of negative changes and promote that of positive changes.

Without knowledge and understanding of the business process as it affects business management, management can do little to help the business survive, much less grow and be successful.

No one book—or many books, for that matter—is going to make business management into experts in all business fields. Yet, management cannot view business as walking through a strange dark alley with unknown dangers lurking everywhere. In business there are few mysteries and a lot of hard facts.

Management must be able to identify and understand the facts. It must know how to listen to its business, its industry, and the economy. It must be aware of all the things that can affect the business and its success.

Management must know whether or not it can respond to changes and needs it identifies, and whether it can effectively respond without help. It has to know the kind of help it needs and what it can expect. And it must know how to maximize its own resources as well as resources from the outside.

In short, management must understand what business is all about.

In this free enterprise system, all can enter into business, and, most important, all can avail themselves of the necessary knowledge and understanding and find the kind of help to give them a good chance of succeeding in business. Those who take advantage of all opportunities to learn and to expand their awareness and understanding are better prepared for a business career.

There is little excuse for not learning and for not becoming aware, knowledgeable, and businesswise. Learning is a function of management that must be taken seriously.

If management does not make continuous efforts to learn more about the business process—about managing, kinds of businesses, its industry, and all other business concerns—it is not performing its functions and will endanger the success of the business.

Management does not have to know all the answers, but it should know the questions. It should be able to identify problems and problem areas and know when they need immediate attention. If management does not have the answers, it can find them.

There are libraries full of books. There are trade magazines and journals. There are government agencies offering all kinds of business assistance and service. There are business schools in colleges and universities that offer business counsel and aid.

Management must also learn to move itself.

Each business must pull its own wagon. Do not expect others to pull it for you. They may help you over the bumps and cracks, lead you through heavy traffic, and show you the way, but it is you who must move the business along on its way to success. Do not pull your business like a horse with blinders but like a thinking man or woman, learning, as you go, to steer your own course, to get over the trouble spots by yourself, and to make it easier to pull along.

A business manager is a beast of burden, and those burdens never really lighten—they just change. And small-business owners or managers are the noblest beasts of burden because they contribute to the entire economy and society through their efforts, despite the fact that their efforts are seldom praised or even appreciated. They have tremendous resources and talents that can be applied to the benefit of all businesses.

As a manager develops his or her skills and understanding, some aspects of the burden lighten but others may become heavier. As operations improve, and the "wagon" rolls along better and more easily, more and more learning must be done to move it along faster and to reach the goals of the business.

Responsibility is always a heavy load.

Once an owner or manager runs away from his or her responsibility, the business suffers. The load stays with you at all times, and it never really grows lighter.Yet, business is an exciting challenge with many rewards, and to the business owner or manager those rewards are worth the effort and the burdens.

Get smart. It all means something only if you receive the rewards and can enjoy them.

Each business is its own wagon, and management must pull it along.

People do not go into business to reduce their burdens. They go into business to trade burdens for rewards. If you only have burdens and no rewards, get out of business, because you have a bad deal.

Rewards come with sound management. Keep your eyes, your ears, and your mind open and seek ways to make it possible for the business to give you the rewards you deserve.

Ask questions. Look for answers. Get help if you need it. Keep your eyes on the reward, but concentrate on the burdens. If you do that, the rewards will come within reach.

Index